C000111997

FREE SPIRITED

HOW MY DAUGHTER HEALED ME FROM THE
AFTERLIFE

SUZANNE FALTER

LOVE & HAPPINESS PUBLISHING

For
Andrea J. Lee
who was there

"You will be in your power when you are overtaken by the light, and you can see everything as an opening to freedom."

Teal's journal
August 3, 2011

CHAPTER ONE

T his story is true. Here is how it began.

It was close to midnight and the house was quiet. Outside in the still Adirondack night, the sound of a lone coyote calling for its pack drifted in through the open window of a young woman named Teal. She closed her eyes as she sat on her bed. And she waited.

Soon the goddesses would be joining her, along with the loving spirit of her deceased grandfather. Teal wasn't sure why he kept showing up, but he did.

She sat with the tattered, red spiral notebook that served as her journal, ready to jot down any words of wisdom she might receive. As usual, she prayed for guidance. Help me with my worries, she invoked. Briefly Teal cataloged them all in her mind.

There was an upcoming urge to travel. Should she head off with her backpack again? And where could she go this time? Was it actually safe to hitchhike by herself in Europe, or possibly in some place more exotic? And if it wasn't, how would she get around? She didn't have a lot of money for trains and buses.

And finally, more importantly, when would she find a boyfriend?

Words and images swam through her mind as the goddesses began their nightly litany.

Everything is falling into place in due time. Your mind and emotions will tell you things, but your body will feel you things, they counseled.

You wanted to go on a vagabonding adventure, they continued. Listen to your body's response.

On and on came the whispered words of encouragement and advice. It was comfort Teal had come to rely upon over the past year.

Eventually a singular thought drifted down from beyond.

Death will come soon.

Teal's eyes snapped open in alarm. What did this mean?

Blankly, she looked around in the darkness of her childhood bedroom, and she felt genuinely afraid. Were her upcoming travel plans too risky? Or was this because she'd had a few drinks the week before? Her neurologist told her that alcohol could be dangerous for her epilepsy. She felt an immediate pang of remorse.

That was it, Teal decided. She would strictly adhere to all her doctor's orders from now on. No more visiting bars. But would that be enough? She returned to her meditation, desperate for more guidance, more information, more answers, more help.

That is when she heard Johno, the grandfather who'd died before she was born. She felt his love clearly as she listened to his counsel.

Be strong. You can do this.

Teal had no idea what he was talking about. But she was comforted all the same.

One night several months before her death, my daughter took me aside. At that moment I was packing up my apartment to move, and I had little interest in any of her good suggestions. Still Teal prevailed, just as she usually did.

"Take a minute and watch the sunset tonight, Mom," she suggested. "It's so incredible from these windows."

My apartment had a sweeping view of the western half of San Francisco, over which the great Pacific sunsets rose like a majestic queen. I was full of hubris then and thought my time was much too valuable to spend on a sunset.

"Honey, I'm just so busy," I protested.

Teal gave me a disapproving look. "Mom. Have you ever watched a sunset in the year and a half that you've lived here?"

I was silent.

"Just as I thought," said Teal, shaking her head. "Come on, Mom. Just do it. And watch the whole thing, right up until dark. No sneaking away."

She started out the door, then stopped and turned around.

"Call me when you've done it," she added. "I'll be waiting."

The door closed with a click.

I sighed. Unpacked boxes were scattered on the floor around me. Watching the sunset was about the last thing I wanted to do. Still, something that night made me stop and listen to my daughter.

I quieted my usual frenetic self, sat down, and waited. After a few moments, the sunset began.

A subtle shell pink spread out from the horizon as the molten lump of the sun slipped away.

I relaxed. I felt myself soften and let go. So much had weighed on my mind lately, impossible things like whether I should be moving in with the woman I called my partner. I knew it would be a fiasco, but still I kept on plodding steadily forward, ignoring the many red flags waving wildly all around me.

The sunset spread throughout the entire sky, deepening pink, radiating peach, then blue, purple, even streaks of green. Every color of the rainbow passed before my eyes in this massive light show at the edge of the city. But I couldn't truly feel the beauty of the sunset.

Not yet.

At that moment, my life was a mess. The successful spiritual marketing business I'd come to San Francisco to build was suddenly ending. What stood in its place was something far less reliable and even downright sketchy. I called it The Spiritual Diet and I honestly had no idea what it was.

I just knew, from all my years as a marketer that this brand would sell. And I knew I was charismatic enough and supposedly spiritual enough in the front of the room to sell it.

Yet outside these windows was the true expansion, the purest wonder of God. Outside these windows was the spirituality before which we are dwarfed. As Teal so rightly suggested.

Outside these windows was my salvation, but it would take the worst crisis of my life for me to understand this.

I would have to fall apart completely and, thus, be completely reborn.

I sat on the couch as the sunset spread just beyond my reach. The buildings of the Castro and the Haight grew peach, then pink, then rose, their windows iridescent glimmers in the sunglow.

A small part of me was still awake enough to see what Teal was showing me—that I had become lost in a cloud of delusion. I sighed and closed my eyes and tried not to feel the pounding of my own heart.

What in God's name had I done to my life?

The sunset continued, consuming the sky in its own sweet time. I eyed the boxes all around me, empty and waiting. Dully I regarded the sky one more time; I really couldn't watch a sunset.

Not now.

I got up and mechanically began to fill boxes. I had to stay busy. Keeping my head down, I glanced over once more at the sunset. The deepening red sky now filled the corners of the windows in a triumphant climax. A blanket of lavender-gray fog had begun to roll in around Twin Peaks.

Tears sprang into my eyes as I kept on packing. I couldn't let my heart catch up with me; I just couldn't. There was far too much to lose to tell the truth in this particular moment. If these last, pathetic vestiges of love and respect—the empty framework I called my life—slipped away, then I would be lost and utterly alone.

Alone, that is, except for Teal.

Pack, I thought. *Just pack.* Head down, I continued as tears poured down my face.

The phone rang a moment later. It was Teal. "So?" she asked. "Did you watch it?"

"Magnificent," I said, trying to sound as normal as possible. No one could know that I was falling apart. Not even my daughter. "Thank you, honey," I heard myself say. "Thanks for making me do that."

"You're welcome, Mom," she said lightly. "Love you."

But of course, Teal knew I was falling apart, and that I needed to. She knew far more for her twenty-two years than most people learned in entire lifetimes. This light-filled being, whose deepest love was her love for others, would soon be returned to dust. And I would become humble again in ways I couldn't currently imagine.

Teal was my healer, though at the time I was too blind to see it. First, she would have to die. Then I would, as well. So we would both be reborn in completely different ways.

The path to the true magnificence had already begun.

CHAPTER TWO

I t was a hot, sunny morning in the old section of Marrakesh, the place Teal had ultimately decided to travel to next.

Teal and her friend Sean hoisted their backpacks on their backs and made their way down the tiled corridors of the hostel. Past the bright blue painted doors, past the row of towels drying on the ornate balcony, underneath the classic Moroccan archways they went.

They'd arrived a few nights before, after spending several days in Italy. She'd gotten the idea for the trip a week earlier, back when they were both in Upstate New York. Her friend Sean was about to start a junior year abroad. So why not see the world a little first?

Now that she had some money in her pocket from her work as a waitress, the world was Teal's oyster, and she was eager to share it with an old friend. In her mind, Morocco was only a quick plane ride away. She'd been there once before when she was ten, accompanying her father on a video shoot. On that trip, she'd been minded on the set by crew and cast, which included a loving group of Moroccan prostitutes who spoke no English and decorated her arms and hands with henna tattoos.

As Sean stepped up to the front desk to check out, Teal suddenly dropped her pack behind him. In a panicked voice, she told him she *had to go lie down immediately. She knew the warning signs—the first deep, shaking waves of anxiety followed by a strangely disconnected feeling of floating. They were unmistakable.*

Furiously, Teal ran for the stairs and the room they'd just left.

Sean followed anxiously. When he reached her, Teal was lying on the bed. Quickly she told him she was in the early stages of having a seizure and would need to lie still for a while. Then she filled him in on what to do in case she seized, explaining how to position her head, and to call for an ambulance immediately if it became a full grand mal seizure. She also instructed him to convince the hostel staff that she was fine and just needing a little rest. Then Teal fell fast asleep.

Sean sat by her side for the next twenty-four hours, nervously watching and waiting. Occasionally, she would stir but never quite wake up. Mid-morning the following day, Teal finally opened her eyes.

"It was as if she was reborn," Sean later recalled. "She was filled with an unbelievable energy.... I can remember a passion in her eyes that I had never seen in anyone before as she talked about her experience."

Teal described how she had been visited energetically by two massive snakes. As she lay there on the bed, they wrapped themselves around her, infusing her body with a bright, healing light. Bolts of white-hot energy surged through her, cutting away the old and instilling the new.

When Teal woke up, she believed something life changing had just happened to her.

"Never have I witnessed someone so spiritually moved. Honestly, it was inspiring," Sean recalled. Teal spent much of their remaining week together journaling about the experience and trying to learn more about the healing snakes. It was possible, she believed, she might be able to heal others.

A week later, she skyped me.

"Guess what," she said. "You remember that healing gift I keep thinking I'm going to get?"

For the previous eight months, Teal had insisted that "something really big" was going to happen to give her the ability to heal people. I listened indulgently, not quite believing what she was talking about.

"Well, I think I got it in Morocco," Teal remarked.

A few days later, she wrote in her diary that the occasional seizures that came with her epilepsy were a blessing, giving her "connection with the Divine."

What do I do with this gift? she wrote in her journal, and her spiritual guides promptly answered.

You will see, they said, when the time is right.

ONE YEAR LATER

The night that my daughter collapsed began happily enough.

I lounged on the side-by-side beds in the chic boutique hotel with my old friend Andrea, in for a brief visit from Vancouver. It was a rare treat that Andrea actually made it to San Francisco, so I traveled into the city to hang with her for a night.

We were laughing and gossiping just as we always did when the phone suddenly rang. It was nearly midnight. No one ever called me at midnight.

"Who the hell is this?" I asked jauntily as I inspected the screen. *Restricted* read the caller ID. I answered, curious more than anything else.

"Are you the mother of Margaret Teal Barns?" asked the disembodied voice on the other end.

Within less than a moment, I was racing down the hotel stairs and out through the hotel lobby, desperately looking for a taxi. And that is when everything began to change.

In the last few months, my entire life had imploded. I'd ended my business, crawled out of the toxic relationship I was in, and moved out of the brand-new apartment that came with it.

At this point, I was living here and there just north of the Bay Area with nothing more than my car, a few suitcases and my laptop. My belongings were in storage, and I was temporarily housed in a hippie town called Sebastopol. Somehow I'd also managed to pick up another love interest—a woman I'll call Rita.

It felt like my life had come completely undone. But as it turns out, the unraveling had only just begun.

That night Rita and I went to dinner at a Peruvian restaurant in San Francisco's North Beach district. By now Teal was living in San Francisco and had decided to stay for a while. She'd even gotten her own apartment and, for reasons I didn't quite understand, just quit her job.

The next day she was to begin taking an eclectic bunch of classes at San Francisco's City College—everything from Astronomy to Native American History & Culture. It was a curriculum she'd designed herself; her first official foray onto the path of becoming a healer. This had become her focus since she gave up a budding career in Austin, Texas singing the blues a year earlier.

"It's just what I want to do," Teal explained, though she couldn't say what sort of healer she might become. In fact, she had no idea.

Teal drifted into the restaurant an hour late that night. She was otherworldly, and more beautiful than ever with her long, honeyed hair, her blue eyes the color of an ocean wave, her creamy skin, and her lovely high cheekbones. Teal's clothing was simple—often just jeans and a T-shirt or a blouse, a pair of Keds or flats. She seldom wore make up. Hers was a beauty that was entirely unselfconscious.

The twenty-something guys at the next table shifted and

looked up as she joined us. One of them smiled at her. She did not appear to notice.

It was not like Teal to be so late, not at all. Shortly before she arrived, I texted her, asking where she was. A text she sent back didn't quite make sense.

Prob be there in ten ha!

After she arrived, she was vague about what had made her late. She couldn't really say. More significantly, she was extremely quiet. Her usual verve was gone.

Teal couldn't tell me, for instance, that she had just dropped in on her dear friend and fellow musician, an older Spanish man named Nacho. Before walking out the door, she suddenly sat down at the piano and sang her favorite song, *Wagon Wheel*, including the final lines.

If I die in Raleigh
At least I will die free

After the song ended, Teal gave him an extra-long hug, uncharacteristic for her.

Then she simply rose and walking to the door, she said, "We'll play together again soon." Then she left.

That night Teal tucked into her dinner with gusto and had little to say to either Rita or me. We tried to bring up topic after topic of conversation, all of which fell flat. I watched my daughter and studied her strange behavior. I wondered if she was feeling shy in front of my new girlfriend.

In my eagerness to make the dinner with Rita go well, Teal's epilepsy didn't even occur to me. Nor did my mind go to a conversation we'd had only the day before. She'd called while I was preparing for a few dinner guests, and in my customary too-busy fashion, I tried to put her off.

"No, Mom," she'd said insistently. "You need to listen to me." I stopped and sat down, phone in hand.

Teal then described the last three or four days as 'not good.'

"I think I'm going to have a really big seizure," she explained. "But maybe it's just more panic attacks…" Her voice trailed off uncertainly. The anti-seizure drugs she took always made it hard for her to tell.

She refused my offer to take her to see the neurologist. "They're just going to change my meds, and I like them, Mom," she said. "They make me feel closer to God."

Something in that moment made me ask an improbable question—one so strange I didn't even understand why I was asking it.

"What about this experience fits your life purpose?"

Teal paused for a moment. "Well, I know I'm meant to heal women and girls who have anxiety and panic. So, yeah, that's probably it." She gave a sign of relief. "Thanks, Mom," she said. "I feel so much better now."

Yet here I was now, sitting in the restaurant the very next night with my spaced-out daughter, and her imminent seizure was far from my mind.

Silently, Rita and I watched her eat.

Soon a speaker took the podium and began describing the life and work of the jungle shamans. Then he got to the part about how shamans travel the space between the waking world and the afterlife.

Suddenly, Teal swiveled in her seat and stared at me intently, a look of awe and astonishment on her face. It was the first time I'd seen her react to anything since she'd arrived.

I nodded, to indicate I got it. But Teal repeated this action several more times, whenever the speaker mentioned the shaman's link to the afterlife. Each time she looked at me keenly, her face lit with a childlike amazement. Her eyes were wide with wonder.

Teal said nothing, but the expression on her face was clear, as if to say, *Are you getting this, Mom? Are you getting this? Like…for real?*

The lecture passed quickly, and my mind turned to my next

event. I was off to meet Andrea and there was little time to waste. Without another thought, I secured Teal a ride home with a friend of Rita's. Then we all said goodbye.

I still remember that last, precious hug vividly. Teal's cool, thick hair nestled next to my cheek. I could feel the smaller mass of her body next to mine, and her sweet arms circled around me.

"Bye, Mom," she said simply. "I love you."

Then I was gone, out the door, my mind spinning off in an entirely different direction.

———————

At this point, I would like to say I glanced back and saw my daughter standing in the half-light of the restaurant, looking around for her ride home. Or that I had a pang of doubt about leaving her in her strange state, and so I stopped and returned to the restaurant.

I would like to say that I immediately drove her home myself. Or better yet, to the nearest Emergency Room.

But I didn't.

Instead, my mind stayed squarely focused on my own plans. I wasn't even remotely worried about my daughter. I kissed Teal and Rita goodbye and hurried on into the night.

After we parted ways, Rita's friend dropped Teal off and watched her weave unsteadily up the stairs to her apartment. Assuming Teal was just a drunk girl now delivered home safely, she drove on.

Teal walked into her bedroom and took off her coat. Then she went into the bathroom and locked the door. At that point it's not clear what happened. Something, which even the San Francisco Medical Examiner could not explain, caused her to have a complete cardiac arrest.

Teal's lifeless body now lay sprawled, face down, in an empty bathtub.

In the next room, her housemate Adam lay on his bed

listening to his headphones. He was barely aware Teal had come home.

Ten to twenty minutes later, Adam attempted to use the bathroom and found the light on and the door locked. There was no response to his knocks. In the moments that followed he deliberated about what to do next.

Was this an emergency or not? Should he break open the lock? What if Teal just needed to be alone for personal reasons and so she wasn't answering?

He tried phoning Teal but her cell phone ringer was off. They'd only shared the apartment for a few months, and he really didn't know her that well.

Should he try to intervene?

Back and forth Adam went in his mind until finally, some moments later, he jimmied the door open and found Teal face down in the bathtub. She had no heartbeat and no pulse. She appeared to be dead.

The EMTs came within moments and managed to restart Teal's heart. Then they rushed her still unconscious body off to San Francisco General. There was no sign of any alcohol or drugs in her blood. She hadn't tried to take her own life.

At age twenty-two, Teal had simply…died.

For the first time.

CHAPTER THREE

A*fter she left Morocco with Sean, Teal traveled solo down Italy's Amalfi coast. It was a place that she'd discovered on a backpacking trip the previous year.*

One sunset evening as she was out walking, she came upon a cemetery.

> *It was white marble and really amazing…overlooking the sea, cliffs, mountains, and towns,* she wrote in her journal. *So, I chose to go in and meditate, and I got this: 'Open your heart, open your soul and be.'*
>
> *The whole 'be' thing really made an impact on me. I realized in life I am never really there. I tend to be thinking about the future or past or something someone said instead of being in the moment and taking it in for all its beauty.*
>
> *After this meditation, I knew I had been transformed because I looked out over the ocean and mountain scene in front of me and started to cry. I was really able to take it all in.*
>
> *I finally realized how blessed I am to be here, and how many beautiful things there are here.*

Teal sat there a little longer as the night in front of her began to unfold. It was blue and beautiful, and seemed to expand to infinity as she watched.

She was learning to just be.

———

Autopilot is the word I would use when describing that first awful night, or perhaps bewilderment. I felt as alone as I ever have, moving through steps, decisions, a vast sea of utter strangeness in a life that suddenly went from being mine to being something else entirely.

As the cab hurtled through the dark toward San Francisco General Hospital, I felt my complete and total powerlessness. No matter how fast the taxi raced, I couldn't save my daughter now. There was nothing to be done.

Shakily, I called Larry, my former husband of twenty-five years and Teal's dad. It was after 3 AM in upstate New York, and his cell phone rang and rang.

I hung up, dialed the house phone, and began leaving a message: "Wake up. We're having a medical emergency with Teal. Call me…"

Larry picked up. "What? What is it?" he asked sleepily.

At that moment, his voice dropped in like a reassuring anchor, something I could cling to as I began the long, tumbling descent down to the very bottom of my life. The fear that had been shrieking through my body now settled into my belly like a stone. Thank God we'd had an amicable divorce, I thought to myself.

"You and Luke are going to have to fly out here in the morning," I told him. "I don't know what's happened but she's in a coma in critical condition. She had a cardiac arrest. Expect to be here for a while."

I didn't envy him the task of telling our eighteen-year-old son. Luke and Teal were as close as brother and sister could be.

Larry struggled to understand. "Okay, okay," he finally said. "Call when you know more."

The cab pulled up to the hospital. I thrust a twenty at the driver and ran for the door. I rushed to the desk and started explaining who I was. At that moment, a social worker appeared and hustled me past the swinging doors into the ER.

All hell seemed to be breaking loose as I entered; there was electric intensity all around me.

"Thank God we got her back," the social worker said, as we hurried along. "She had another cardiac arrest when she arrived. So far we have no cause."

"Did you know Teal is epileptic?" I asked.

The social worker looked at me. "That could explain a lot," she said. The social worker led me to a small, private waiting room away from the fray. It was a muted room in institutional green. Prints of sailboats hung on the walls.

It was the kind of place where people get very bad news.

Nothing in motherhood prepares you for the moments when you sit alone on the cold vinyl couch, anticipating the worst possible news about your child. A kind police officer brought me a bottle of water.

A motherly looking Black woman, an administrator, came in to get Teal's paperwork signed and I burst into tears. She put her arms around me, and then surprisingly, she, too, began to cry as we hugged each other.

"I know how it is," the woman assured me. "I know how it is." Her body was big and comforting and for a moment we just hung on to each other. She clearly knew things, terrible things, that I was just on the cusp of learning.

Wiping her tears away, she handed a manila envelope with the contents of Teal's wallet.

Shakily, I opened the envelope and looked inside: four dollars, Teal's driver's license, a Clipper transit card, and two stickers saying: *These Come from Trees.*

Every so often Teal would paste one of these on a paper

towel dispenser in a public bathroom, her form of environmental protest. A hollow place formed in my chest now, an aching, an uncertainty. I recognized it somehow. It was the shadow of Death.

Finally, the attending physician came in. He was a weary-looking man in maroon scrubs who'd clearly delivered a lot of bad news in his life.

"It's rough," he began. Then he added for emphasis, "Very rough."

The physician went on to tell me that Teal had suffered a cardiac arrest and was without a heartbeat for 15 to 30 minutes before her heart was shocked back to life again. She'd had a second cardiac arrest when she arrived at the hospital, from which her heart was also restarted. She remained in a coma. Since the brain can only survive without a heartbeat for four to seven minutes, her condition was grave.

It was likely that Teal had sustained extensive brain damage.

Yet the protocol now was treat her as if they could save her life, and as if her brain damage was minimal. There was still a tiny, miraculous chance that she could somehow emerge from this, because the exact length of time she was without a heartbeat was unknown.

Somehow Teal's pupils still responded to light, and she'd managed to breath some of the time without the ventilator. These were both positive—even amazing—signs. The doctor assured me they would do everything they could.

He walked me to the elevator. "Why don't you ride upstairs with her?" he gently suggested.

I stepped into an elevator going up with the heavily encased figure on a gurney that was my daughter. My daughter, who I'd had eaten dinner with only three hours earlier.

A hush fell over the four nurses and technicians gathered around her.

"It's Mom, honey," I said to her expressionless body. "I'm here and you're doing great. These people are taking incredibly good care of you. They know exactly what to do. And Dad and Luke are on their way."

All was silent for a moment.

I continued, my voice quivering. "Just hang in there, honey. We're doing everything we can to help you."

The doors opened and they hustled her off.

My daughter disappeared behind swinging metal doors.

I stood looking at Teal on the hospital bed before me. The machines of the trauma unit whirred and beeped around us, a strange, barren symphony of sounds.

Her arms and legs were swaddled in layers of thermal padding; wires snaked out from behind her muted blue hospital gown. An IV poked out of each hand above her chipped purple nail polish. An array of monitors played overhead.

Only her head and her feet were plainly visible. Her eyes were half-open; unseeing. I touched her feet and suddenly her eyelids sprung open wide and she looked at me for an instant. Her expression was one of complete and total shock. The whites flashed wide around her beautiful teal-colored eyes before they closed again.

Once more she appeared to be sleeping.

"It was only a reflex," commented the nurse seated nearby who was monitoring Teal. "It's normal."

This was a new normal for which I was not prepared. And yet, as I stood there looking at her, the sense that this *was* normal—even to be expected—settled over me. In a nanosecond, I understood. Teal would die, and I would be delivered to an entirely new life. Perhaps even the life of my dreams.

My mind scrambled, trying to understand.

It was as if a team of heavenly archangels had parted the curtains for one split second, and I could glimpse what lay ahead. It involved helping people—many people—in a real, intimate way well beyond anything I'd ever known before.

But first it involved becoming a much kinder person. A better person. A person like my daughter.

This was the cliff I'd been waiting patiently to jump off of for as long as I could remember. I realized now that I'd prepared for this moment my entire life, though I'd never known exactly what it was.

This was the beginning of everything, yet it made no sense at all.

As the night wore on, I sat by Teal's side. Every so often I would stroke her cheek or her arm and tell her what a good job she was doing. Even in her coma, I reasoned that some part of her could hear me. Her body was already like some sort of large, inanimate object, a robot on the worktable, guts wide open and under repair.

"This must be so hard for you," said the attending nurse, "not knowing…"

She was referring to the unthinkable that had not been named, of course. That Teal might die. Or worse, that Teal might live the rest of her life in a vegetative state, unable to do the simplest of things, not quite alive yet not quite dead.

For one as joyous and free through her life as Teal, this was simply unthinkable.

"Life is change," I heard myself say to the nurse. I had no idea where this statement came from.

As I sat there, I felt complete surrender. I was no longer in control; I was simply moving to God's rhythm. My soul had already done the math. This was an inevitable moment in her life and mine, like a perfect storm.

I knew the truth. Whether Teal lived or died, the less I resisted, the better this would go.

I took a long, shaking breath and probed, with the tiniest of tendrils, what life without her might be like. My mind came up blank.

Unreasonable reason whirred and sputtered into action. *Teal could wake up! Her eyes might snap open, and she might look at me at any moment. Conscious! Alive! Almost her old self again!*

She might wake up and groggily say, "Hi, Mom! What's up?"

But deep in my heart, the knowing was already there. Our souls had walked this road many times before and there was no going back. This time she would die, and I would be reborn. It was simply the way it was.

I called my assistant, Darcee. It was 4:30 AM in Boston. She picked up, reliable as ever.

"Suzanne?" she croaked. Her voice was muddled with sleep.

"Teal's had a cardiac arrest," I said. "She's in a coma." Then I began to cry. "She may…she may…" I could not say the words.

Darcee listened silently.

"She may *die*," I finally blurted out.

"Oh my God!" Darcee burst. Then she also began to cry.

The reality was sinking in now. The word had to be uttered, because without it none of this would make sense. The puzzle pieces were rapidly whirring and clicking into place.

Rita reappeared that night, bringing helpful things I might need, and the two of us attempted a nap in a nearby waiting room. Then Adam, Teal's housemate, showed up as well, with a bag of Teal's meds and supplements for toxicology testing.

In the bleakest hours that first night, the three of us hung on to each other, alternately praying, crying, and trying to convince ourselves this was actually happening.

Teal's father and her brother arrived the next afternoon from the East coast. The three of us sat by her side for the next five days. Teal, meanwhile, lingered between worlds.

We each had our different hopes and prayers. Larry imagined she could rise up and be the one magical patient to survive this thing. ("It's happened," a nurse told him. "Not very often, but it has.") Her brother Luke sat by her side simply waiting, in tears sometimes but other times in a kind of patient grace that is his gift in this world.

His heartbreak was the most tragic piece of this entire experience for me. After arriving at the hospital, he pulled his small tribute to Teal out of his backpack: a four-leaf clover packed in a wet napkin.

Teal could find four-leaf clovers wherever she went, which she always shared with whomever was by her side. Evidently, she had taught her magic to her brother. Luke had picked the clover from the yard as they were leaving to fly West.

He also brought the teddy bear she had given him years earlier; it was ratty and a little threadbare. Carefully, Luke placed it under Teal's bandaged hand, arranging the IV line over it. Her limp fingers rested lightly on the bear's fur.

As for me, I simply sat; at first unwilling to comprehend the inevitable, but then more and more willing as the days went on. This I source to something that happened the second night after Teal's collapse.

She was still in an induced coma, and on paralytic drugs to keep her body completely still. Her heartbeat had somehow mysteriously stabilized. In an extraordinary measure, her doctors moved her from Cardiac ICU into the Neuro Trauma unit, where they could focus on the swelling in her brain.

A monitor had been surgically implanted into her scull to measure the growing pressure inside her head as her injured brain expanded and contracted. Test after test continued. Teal was now on a ventilator full time. The prognosis was not good.

And yet suddenly on the second night, in the 3 AM gloom of my Best Western hotel room, there she was. I woke up to a light, lemony, charged energy that filled my senses. It was joyful, ebullient, and it said, *Hey, Mom!*

I blinked, uncertain of what was happening. *It couldn't be Teal…could it? Was such a thing even possible?*

I decided this was a dream, but then I listened eagerly. For here was Teal, more radiant than ever, her presence fizzy with effervescence. I grasped for whatever I could get of her. "Honey? Is that you?" I asked silently.

Mmm-hmm, I heard her say. Suddenly I felt tingly, alive. Electric. Like her energy was fizzing up inside of me.

"What are you doing? What's going on?" I asked, struggling to understand what was happening.

I'm trying to reconcile my heart and my soul, calmly replied the voice in my head.

Over at the hospital, Teal remained in a coma. For the last two days, her pupils had continued to dilate, and her heart had beaten steadily on its own without interruption, as if her body was still trying to get a grip. Which in and of itself was miraculous.

"Are you going to die?" I asked.

Haven't decided yet…. I'll let you know. Then her voice added a few more words for emphasis. *Don't rush me.*

This was so Teal.

She was always one for moving slowly and thoughtfully— unless she felt moving fast and recklessly. She was a total free spirit in her short life; one who would accept no reining in. Especially from me, with my tendency to hurry everyone around me to hop to my agenda.

"Okay," I said. "Just let me know, honey."

'Kay, I heard her say.

Then she disappeared.

I sighed. Her touch of brilliance ignited my consciousness. I felt clean and jubilant. I wanted to jump out of bed and wake the others.

"Teal's here!" I wanted to proclaim. "She's not going anywhere, even if she does die. She's around us all the time. It's all going to be okay!"

My former husband and my son slept on unaware in the next bed.

I stopped for a moment, puzzling over her choice of words. *Reconciling her heart and her soul.* What did that mean, exactly?

I had no idea, but I was sure I would soon find out.

CHAPTER FOUR

I n the four days that followed Teal's collapse, her physical presence steadily declined. Each day there were more tests, more probes, more procedures, and more papers to sign.

The margin of her life grew slimmer and slimmer.

A chaplain appeared—a kind woman with gray hair and a red thread tied around her wrist that subtly identified her as a practicing Buddhist. She quietly took up her position by Teal's bed, monitoring the spiritual well-being of the situation.

On the third day, I found myself silently asking Teal if she'd made up her mind yet and the answer came quickly.

Yeah. I'm going to cross over.

There it was, plain and simple. There was no drama about it, nor was there any regret. It was just a simple statement of fact, an irrefutable truth I'd have to get used to.

On the fourth day, I consulted with the chaplain. We went for a little walk around the hospital floor, away from Larry, Luke and I told her what I had heard. The chaplain let out an involuntary sob. For she, too, had fallen for Teal.

Then pulling herself together, the chaplain gave me good counsel. Together we agreed this was not information I needed to share with anyone; it was for me at this point. Then we were left to marvel at the spiritual unfolding that was happening all around us.

Both of us recognized we were in the clutch of Grace.

Later that same afternoon, I found myself sitting alone with Teal. I held my daughter's lifeless hand in my own and closed my eyes. Her hand was as warm and tender, as if she might just be napping. Teal hadn't moved a muscle, nor was she likely to. But in that instant, something extraordinary happened.

I felt a spiritual presence, perhaps Grace itself, move through her hand into my own—for that is the only possible description of what happened.

At that moment, a surreal surge of joy poured into my body, like a thousand-watt Christmas tree. A broad, involuntary smile spread across my face. Then a warm melting presence entered my body.

I felt completely surrendered to bliss.

But this time, it wasn't just Teal's energy I was sensing. Instead, it seemed to be a heavenly chorus of angels, archangels and who knows what else calling her forth as I sat by her side and watched. Perhaps even her friends Jesus, Brahma and Allah were there as well.

It was as if her soul detached from her body at that moment and moved out into the ethers. So Teal went, merging with the Universe, with me, and every other living thing.

The rush of extreme joy was palpable. In that moment of witnessing, I felt the purest presence of God that I had ever known.

Remarkably, Teal didn't physically die at that moment. Her heart continued to beat, and the ventilator continued its mechanical whoosh as if nothing had happened at all.

Yet, in an instant, the sweet sparkling essence that was Teal was gone. An inert figure lay on her bed. She had become nothing more than a place marker.

Larry and Luke returned to the room a few moments later but I did not tell them what I had witnessed. Instead, I went for a walk around the hospital. Down the corridors I walked, aimlessly, looking for…something. For what, I wasn't exactly sure.

I saw shuffling homeless people. I saw intent medical students and preoccupied doctors. I saw weary family members and achingly pregnant women, small children fluttering around them like fireflies.

As I gazed at these strangers, I found myself seeing right into their very core, as if I knew each one of them intimately. For this one brief moment of my life, my heart opened wide.

I, too, had been transformed that afternoon. For what I felt now was pure, unadulterated, unconditional love for everyone and everything. It scared me. Yet it also filled me with a quiet joy.

I came to rest in a small corridor not far from the Neuro-Trauma Unit. I pulled Teal's cell phone from my pocket, thinking I would call some of her friends. But instead, I found myself looking at a homeless man who was standing just down the hall. I considered speaking to him, but I stopped myself.

Instead, I called Teal's friend Nacho. Nacho answered quickly. "Hey Teal!" he began.

Lowering my voice, I quickly explained who I was and why I was calling. I hung up a moment later and brushed the tears from my face. Having to tell her friends the news gutted me every time.

The homeless man was still there, watching me. He'd been listening to my conversation. I stood up. Then almost involuntarily, I went to him.

"I got kids," he said as I approached.

I nodded. We were quiet for a moment. "My daughter's dying," I said.

"Yeah," he nodded.

"Do you have a daughter?" I asked. I had no idea where this question had come from.

"Yes, I do," he said eagerly. "I know I got to go see her. I got to go *see* that girl," he repeated for emphasis. "I left when she was little, but I can see her now, right? I got to just go see her, don't I?"

We looked at each other.

"You do," I affirmed.

"Okay," said the homeless man, giving my arm a pat. "You take care of yourself, now."

"Thank you," I said. "You too."

I took his hand and squeezed it.

In the days that followed, the dance of death began. Each step felt so purposeful and pure, and each moment became sacred as my daughter moved toward her physical death.

My conversations with the ethereal Teal continued, and now she made requests. She had a lot to say from the afterlife. Teal made it abundantly clear that not a thing in the world was bothering her, now that she was safely, jubilantly, on the other side.

The rest of us mortals, however, were going to have to work out our shit.

For one thing, Teal had ideas about her memorial, which she let me know, wordlessly, in no uncertain terms. It would be held at the family house, and the entire town would be invited. Friends would come and build an altar together. Al Green's "Love & Happiness" would be the closing song.

And there would be a lot of desserts. Because if there was one thing Teal loved in life, it was dessert.

Patiently, we waited for her stone, silent body to die. On the sixth day, Dr. Singh, the attending physician, delivered the news. A small circle of us stood in the hallway outside of Teal's hospital room.

"We have finally been able to look at the CAT scan," she began. "Her brain is…well…." Dr. Singh shook her head, words failing her. "No one can live like this," she finally said.

Now my bravery finally crumbled. It was as if my knees suddenly gave out from under me. "So we will have to let her go," I said, as weeping overtook me. Larry and Luke began to cry, too.

The doctor took us into a small room, and then she held me as I sobbed and sobbed into her shoulder. Her kindness was all encompassing, and I could feel genuine love and compassion surrounding me. A younger man, a Scottish doctor, did his best to console Larry and Luke.

There was nothing more to be said. The bottom had finally, officially dropped out.

Moments later, I asked the medical team to gather with us and bless Teal's life. I sensed this was something new for them. They glanced at each other a little awkwardly as they took each other's hands.

We stood in a circle around her bed—the nurses, Dr. Singh, and anyone else who was present. Together for one brief, sterling moment in the neuro-trauma unit, in spite of our beliefs, our differences, and our appointed jobs, we all prayed for Teal's soul. And we thanked her for gracing us with her presence in this life. Then we stepped aside as the medical team quietly set to work.

In the hours that passed, they took Teal off the drugs that had controlled the swelling of her brain. They turned off the overhead cranial pressure monitors that had been so closely watched, and removed the thermal wraps from her body, and the bandaging and EEG wires that had covered her head.

It was time for Teal to drift slowly, surely to her death.

Her beautiful, dark-honey hair once again cascaded again around her shoulders, and her sweet face was utterly still. Lifelessly still. She looked angelic, as if she were simply resting.

There were things to be done now. First, we had to decide whether we would donate Teal's organs. Minutes after we took Teal off life support, a red-headed woman popped her head around the curtain and said a soft hello. She said her name was Rebecca.

Rebecca had a kind, calm efficiency about her. It was obvious she had spent a lot of time around death. She began the delicate dance of exploring whether we would be willing to donate Teal's organs and tissues.

Because of the gentle way in which Teal was dying, her age, and the fact that her heart had regained stability, she was an unusually good candidate. Teal had left no instructions regarding organ donation, but we knew immediately it was the right thing to do. In fact, it was the perfect way to honor Teal's desire to become a healer. But the decision was harder for her brother, who felt naturally protective of his older sister and what was left of her body.

But eventually Luke agreed. He, too, could feel it was the right thing to do.

Given the complexity of arranging the organ donations, there was little time to waste. In the last hour of Teal's life, I sat with an administrator giving a detailed medical history of every last one of her illnesses and injuries. Meanwhile, a nurse was on alert to let me know when the time of her brain death seemed to be drawing near.

Eventually, she appeared in the doorway. "You'd better come now," she said quietly. Walking toward Teal's deathbed, I felt strangely calm.

I stepped through the curtain into her room, and the scene was utterly peaceful. Teal looked no different from before. Larry and Luke held her hands, quietly waiting. Resigned.

I leaned over and placed a long, tender kiss on the side of my daughter's head. *How will I live the rest of my life without you?* I wondered. And then I chased that thought away.

It just didn't seem to be real.

The three of us watched the overhead monitor, transfixed. A pattern of tiny, spidery spikes rose and fell in cadence, their eventual stillness indicating when her brain death would be complete. Together we watched and waited with quiet acceptance of what was, for there just wasn't any other choice.

The moments ticked by. Sacred. Holy. Perfect. Each one was pure—life with nothing added. And so, Teal's death came quietly, almost unremarkably.

She simply drifted away.

Experts on soul deliverance say that very old souls leave the body well before their actual physical death. As if they are making their way back on such a well-traveled path, they simply can't wait to get there. I believe this is was what happened to Teal.

Three days earlier, Larry had had a vision of Teal in a dream. She was standing outside the hospital dressed in her jeans and a simple gray sweatshirt. And she was smiling broadly, letting him know that everything was just fine.

She exuded a happy, peaceful glow and he could feel her contentment. And then she just walked away.

It was later that same day that I felt her joyful spirit rise into the ethers.

It was on that incredible afternoon when so much light and love poured through my own body that I became, for one brief moment, incandescent. The heavens opened in my own small heart, and I could suddenly feel compassion I'd never known before.

In that moment, I fell in love with humanity and with all that is, and I lost my resistance to the very fiber of life. For once my tortured story was no longer interesting to me.

Instead, a fantastic Universal web of truth, beauty and love held me fast in its grip. That afternoon, as I wandered through the hospital, feeling the pain, the joy, the worry and the fear of all I saw, I could hear Teal telling me this was called The Unified Field of Love.

For the first time in my life, I felt myself to be part of something infinitely vast. Gone were all my material concerns. Gone was the need to know how everything would turn out. Instead, I was released into a pure, sweet moment of being, of infinite love.

It was the very same wide-eyed freedom with which Teal lived her life.

I stepped onto the path of my personal redemption, almost eager to learn what would happen next.

Only now did I fully understand. God had come for me, as well.

CHAPTER FIVE

Nine months before her death, Teal flew from Europe to join me in San Francisco. Our agreement was that she would stay with me for two weeks and no longer. Then she would have to move out. Forget the fact that affordable apartments were already few and far between as San Francisco turned into a bustling tech hub.

Another couple was also temporarily in the second bedroom. Teal would have to sleep on the couch. Gamely, she accepted my terms. Meanwhile, she was eager to get to know her two interesting new housemates, Ambujam and Michael, a pair of psychic healers.

Like Teal, the couple had just arrived in the city. Teal declined an offer to follow me back East for a family Thanksgiving and instead chose to spend the next three days sitting around the apartment, talking to her new friends. Later, she described it in her journal.

I didn't leave the house yesterday. Ambujam and Michael and I sat with each other all day and talked about everything spiritual, not spiritual, and beyond. The energy flow was like nothing I've ever experienced before. It was like a continuous exchange, never stopping, bringing amazing transformation with it wherever it went. I know they are my spiritual teachers, and we have been brought together to heal each other.

Last night when I went to bed, I saw the beings all lined up on three sides of my bed, towering over me. They told me they were here to teach me leadership, love, and spiritual oneness. I also got that my activation is beginning.

The following night Teal had a dream in which she stood on the roof of my building. A huge, ethereal palace like the Taj Mahal began to materialize in front of her.

It was really God-like and what I imagine God's palace in the sky looks like, she wrote. *I was a bit scared because I felt like I could fall off the roof. But I also felt entranced and excited by this new thing that I love to see.*

I saw it as the evolution of my psychic gifts. Or spiritual gifts —whatever they might be. At present, I can only see a bit of the big picture, but soon I will see everything.

One week after arriving in San Francisco, Teal wrote the words on Facebook, I surrender.

The following week she found a job as a barista and a couch to sleep on for a while in the Mission.

Elizabeth Kubler-Ross says that when a death happens suddenly, grief begins with shock. That the psyche will only dribble in as much pain as the heart can stand, increasing it gradually over time. I would concur.

My demeanor was remarkably calm that night and in the days following Teal's death. I moved along, one foot in front of another, quietly getting things done in between short, random bouts of intense sobbing.

Larry and Luke stayed in California for several weeks as we

waited for Teal's body to be released from the Medical Examiner and her remains to be cremated. Since the cause of her collapse remained unknown, the authorities chose to be involved. The three of us clung to each other, trying to make sense of what had just happened. All of it seemed patently wrong, except for certain moments when I realized with perfect clarity just how right, how destined Teal's death actually was.

I had no idea why I knew this, but I did.

My friend Andrea, who was with me the night Teal collapsed, returned from Vancouver with her husband Mike and a box of Caribou Cocktail Mix. With a steady, calm resolve, they held our hands and helped us cope. Together we packed up Teal's apartment: her boxing gloves, her guitars, her collection of heart-shaped rocks, her small altar, and her goddess cards. As well as her brand-new, unread copy of *The Tibetan Book of the Dead*.

Packing up her few things took all of an hour. We left her bed for an incoming tenant, and we hauled her other piece of furniture, a broken bureau, down to the street—which is exactly where it had come from in the first place.

Instead of a funeral, we had parties celebrating Teal's life. The first was in San Francisco, a mid-afternoon gathering with bright colors, recordings of her singing the blues, and lots of recollections and desserts.

Teal's guitar lay open in its case, scattered with tiny white flowers and her well-worn, cardboard busking sign that read, *Hi. My name is Teal. Hope you enjoy the show.* ♥ Behind it was an altar where her friends and co-workers laid their offerings and mementos.

Many of her friends told stories about her life that afternoon. There was the street-tough guy who talked about how she kept smiling at him at the gym where they both boxed. When he gave her his practiced street glare, Teal laughed out loud at him and asked, "Why are you looking at me like that?" Not surprisingly, they became fast friends.

Then there was the tearful young woman who held up her own tattered copy of *The Pocket Pema Chodron*, a book Teal had introduced her to. Teal had helped her sort through her problems by reading from the tiny book, she said, as they took breaks together at work.

The memorial was followed by a Native American fire ceremony up in the wine country, along the Petaluma River, an event put on by strangers somehow moved by the story of the beautiful girl who mysteriously dropped dead.

Finally, ten days later, Larry, Luke and I picked up the small black plastic box containing Teal's ashes from a cremator whose last name, not surprisingly, was Love. Meanwhile, the Medical Examiner on her case was a doctor named Christopher B. Happy. Which, knowing my ebullient daughter, was nothing less than perfect.

The cause of Teal's cardiac arrests remained 'pending.' After a thorough examination, Dr. Happy honestly couldn't say what had happened to her.

We drove out to the shores of Ocean Beach at the edge of San Francisco to scatter her ashes in the Pacific. That afternoon, Larry, Luke and I waded into the sea and stood knee-deep in the frigid water, holding the plastic bag containing the dust that was once Teal. It was a beach she loved in a city she adored.

The three of us each took a turn casting her ashes in billowing arcs around us. They surrounded us in plumes of gray dust then, slowing, settled into the water. We watched as the white of her bone chips sank into the ocean and mingled with the sand, wavelet after wavelet rippling over them. I waded out of the freezing water quickly, finding my spot on the beach, but Larry and Luke stood there for a long time, knee-deep in the Pacific, until there was virtually nothing left to see.

All last traces of Teal were now gone.

Somehow we would have to live the rest of our lives without her.

Already, I felt naked, afraid, and utterly alone.

We were on our way to the airport to fly back east for the second memorial when my phone rang. It was a Bay Area healer I knew named Sandy. A few days earlier she'd seen the news on Facebook and called offering help. "Perhaps I could remove Teal's energy blocks as she transitions?" she'd suggested with a note of practicality. I'd almost laughed at the time. But then, this was California, so why wouldn't a spiritual healer show up to clear your daughter's karma as she dies?

As we sat in a clog of traffic that morning on the Bay Bridge, Sandy was now calling with an update. She'd connected with Teal just after she crossed over, she said.

"Immediately it was all joy and light," she recounted. "My sense was that she was in the light and gone." Sandy asked Teal how she could be of service. Right away, she felt several trapped energies and emotions that needed to be released from our ancestral line.

"They felt like serious torment," she added.

Furthermore, she sensed this healing work was specifically a gift from Teal to me—a restoration, and an alignment of our mutual energy fields. At the time this was cryptic to me. But later, when I thought of everything that followed, this step was nothing less than critical.

"There has been a lot of suffering for the women in your line," Sandy explained.

She saw my Great-Grandmother Sibyl, my grandmother Beth and all my other sad and dour ancestors who'd lost babies, had miscarriages, and suffered through stillbirths. Sandy also saw my mother, a suicidal alcoholic who had three miscarriages. Child loss was something of a family legacy that had continued through many generations.

Again and again Sandy cleared the connections, cut the cords, blessed the energies of suffering and struggle and sent them on their way.

In the healing, Teal appeared as a bright, shining star, a soul freshly set free who was gradually gaining strength as her shackles were lifted, one by one. As Teal moved into greater service, I needed to as well, Sandy informed me. It wasn't clear how that service would manifest, but I could feel its force moving through me already. And I knew it was unstoppable.

"Oh, and one more thing," Sandy noted before she hung up. "It was really strange, but at the end of the session, I swear I heard Teal say, 'I'll be back.' Not in some other lifetime, but in this one. And soon."

CHAPTER SIX

I sat in the bathroom of a crowded airplane, 30,000 feet above Earth, trying to sob silently. I'd already cried my way from New York to Las Vegas. Now on the last leg home to San Francisco, I needed to get a grip.

Raw fear pulsed through my body as my plane drew closer to SFO. My former partner was gone. Larry and Luke were gone. Teal was gone. My home was gone. My business was gone, and my former business partner was now in the midst of moving to Los Angeles. Most of the friends I'd made in San Francisco seemed to have disappeared as well, unable to cope with my crisis.

Rita was even gone. I had broken up with her a few days after Teal's death. She'd done her best to offer me kind, loving support in that final week of Teal's life, but suddenly I had no space for it.

There was no question that I needed to be alone now. My entire focus now shifted to healing myself. Now it was just me, my laptop, a few suitcases, and my small, teal-colored car. I was more alone than I had ever been in my life, at one of the worst times in my life. And somehow that seemed right.

There would no longer be Teal's soft shoulder to lean against.

Just as there would be no more phone calls that began with her warm, purring, "Hi Mom…" Or her dear, sad voice breaking with tears, "Oh, *Mom…*" she would begin.

Blowing my nose, I left the lavatory and walked back to my seat, resolved to move ahead no matter what.

I had been stripped clean of that which no longer served me. And I was being redesigned for an entirely different life, the likes of which I could not even begin to fathom. It was seriously time to get my act together. And if I did, something very good would come out of it. That much I knew.

All I had left of my daughter were a few items of her clothing, a lock of her hair, and her red spiral notebook. This well-worn journal had been entirely filled up with her round curving entries, written after each of her meditations in the previous year. She began keeping it after she started receiving small, important-sounding phrases in the silence.

"What should I do with them?" she'd asked me at the time.

"Oh honey, just write them down in a notebook or something," I told her dismissively. I'd assumed they were just a bit of twenty-something existential angst.

Now, however, I clung to this notebook for all I was worth, trying to make sense of each thing she wrote. Her writing described strange, incredible images from meditations—a spinning carrot, a white knight with a benevolent smile, rods of light penetrating her body. All manner of goddesses, everyone from Isis to Green Tara to Kwan Yin were checking in and issuing advice. Even my own long-dead father seemed to be chiming in.

Some of her entries made perfect, even profound sense,

How do I get in touch with my body? Turn off your brain and ask.

And this one, which I loved.

Trust in the Universe and the Universe will trust in you.

Yet others were simply guidance for any twenty-something woman trying to make her way in the world.

You are having trouble loving yourself. You keep blaming yourself for your bad haircut. You are falling into a circle of blame.

I swallowed when I read this because I remembered that particular haircut. I'd pushed her to go to my new stylist in San Francisco, and she'd left in tears, hating how she now looked.

At the bottom of many pages of the notebook Teal had written her personal mantra.

Just be.

Somewhere deep in my gut, I knew that the key to my salvation lay in this well-used notebook. It was as if Teal had left me written-out instructions on how to become that better person I knew I must now become.

I pulled the notebook from my backpack and flipped through its pages. Much of it made no sense to my grief-addled brain. Still, it was a comfort just to hold it, to know that not too long ago, Teal had actually written in it.

San Francisco came into view out the airplane window. The massive red and white spire of the Sutro Tower poked through a fog bank, as did the tops of the Golden Gate Bridge. Sun curled around the edges of the blanket-white fog, warming it like a tea cozy over the city. Beyond it all spread the Pacific, shining and regal.

Here was my home now, my El Dorado. I had an entirely new life to invent. And, somehow, I would get through this, mainly because I had to.

God only knew how it was going to happen.

I'd read online about a room in Petaluma I could rent. Petaluma was a sweet Victorian village in the wine country north of San Francisco, once known for its butter and egg production.

Now it was populated mostly with well-heeled families and retiring boomers. It was also the place where total strangers held Teal's fire ceremony for us. This seemed like an auspicious sign.

When I found the room to rent on Craig's List, a framed picture of an angel hanging over a couch caught my eye. *I could live there,* I thought, based on pretty much nothing.

My housemates would be two women—an older Brit with a crisp, commanding sense of humor, and a young Chinese-American who worked as a medical technician. Together, they could prove an interesting Yin-Yang to my broken-open soul, or so I imagined. No other listings seemed even remotely appropriate.

Shortly after I arrived, I made a beeline there.

Divina, the Brit, showed me around. "This would be your room," she said, motioning to a large sunny space with a small balcony. I walked in and immediately knew that I wanted it. Something about Divina and the sunny bedroom seemed inherently right. *I could heal here,* I thought.

I broke the delicate news that I was freshly grieving. "But I'll try to keep it to myself," I joked.

Divina peered up at me through her wispy bangs. "No worries," she said. "I'm a healer." I didn't give her comment much thought. Yet, as it turned out…she was right.

Divina was a gifted body worker, so on Sunday nights, I lay on her table as she administered to my frozen neck, my stiff knee, and my aching, shredded heart. This involved an inordinate amount of pain and yelling, and sometimes furious crying. But when it was over my various stiff body parts always moved again, and I felt remarkably nimble and free.

Divina told me the spirit of Mary Magdalene joined her when she was healing people. But then this was the kind of thing she often said, and I wasn't in the mood to even remotely believe her. Her story was, of course, fantastic. Apparently, Mary had first dropped in years earlier, waking Divina from a nap.

"Who are you?" she'd asked sleepily from the thrall of sleep. When Mary told her, Divina answered characteristically. "I'm sorry but you are NOT Mary Magdalene." With that the energy withdrew, then barreled back in again, this time flinging open the shutters of the room and sending in the unmistakable shaft of divine light.

I still wasn't sure what to think. But whoever was helping Divina now, it was working for her.

When I collapsed into tears from time to time, Divina would pound on my door relentlessly until I let her in to comfort me, trailed by Ming Yin in her bunny slippers. Divina was like a fierce mother bear, protecting her cubs—even this grieving and somewhat detached housemate.

She bossed me around, rearranged my kitchen shelves, and tried to steal my parking space more than once. But she also made me laugh at the least likely time in my life. And that was an enormous help.

Up until now, I'd heard nothing from Teal since the week of her death. My grief was like a dense cloud that sat on everything in my life, letting in little to no light. I suspected that I'd never hear from her again. Wonderfully, I was mistaken.

Teal's ethereal essence first popped up in the middle of a dream. *Get a Ouija board,* she told me before she disappeared.

A Ouija board. *Really?*

Ouija boards creeped me out. They seemed the domain of giggling pre-teens and truly desperate, slightly unhinged adults. But Teal whispered in my head, telling me to get one, and at this point, I was following all instructions from the afterlife. Meekly, I ordered one from Amazon.

Divina, Ming Yin and I gathered in my room the night it arrived. I lit a few candles and turned the lights low for atmosphere. Divina and I sat across from each other on my chaise lounge, the Ouija board between us. Gently we put our fingers on either side of the DayGlo plastic planchette, reminding each other not to move it.

Nothing happened. "I'm not moving it," joked Divina.

"Yeah, I'm not either," I replied.

At that moment, the planchette began to quiver and then slide slightly to the right. It pointed to the letter 'Y.' Then it stopped. It didn't move again.

"Y? That's all we get?" Divina finally muttered. She seemed annoyed.

The planchette refused to move. Finally, it slid to the bottom of the board and our fingers rode along with it. *Good Bye*, it said.

"Well," Divina sniffed, somewhat haughtily. She got up and walked out of the room.

Ming Yin and I looked at each other. "Do you want to try?" I asked.

"Okay," she said uncertainly. Then she smiled. "Nothing will probably happen," she said.

Ming Yin, the daughter of Chinese immigrants, was just a few years older than Teal had been. There were stilettos in her closet, right alongside the bunny slippers. She had a feisty streak, and a successful job in medicine. I felt protective toward Ming Yin, motherly even. On a whim, I gave her Teal's down quilt after I moved in. It seemed she needed it.

Ming Yin sat across from me and put her fingers on the other side of the planchette. Immediately, a tingling started at the base of my spine. Then a huge bolt of electricity shot straight up my back, urgent and hot.

It was as if I'd put my finger directly into a live socket.

"Oh my God!" I cried as the force field of electricity consumed me and slammed straight into my brain. The surge was so powerful it moved me to tears. "This is incredible!" I moaned, my eyes clamped shut as tears poured down my face. It was one of the most intense things I'd ever experienced in my entire life.

Where in God's name is this coming from?

Back on the Ouija Board, the planchette was going crazy, moving furiously from letter to letter. "I can't… I can't…." I said breathlessly, as I struggled to keep my hands on the speeding planchette.

"Suzanne?" I heard Ming Yin ask in a worried voice. I couldn't answer her. "I'm not moving it! I'm not doing anything, I swear!" she insisted.

I moaned again. The energy that was passing through my body was so huge and relentless, overwhelming. I still couldn't speak. "Hey, what's happening?" Ming Yin now cried.

The planchette zipped around the board, going crazy. "It's spelling something. M ... A .... R .... Y ... M ... A ... G," read Ming Yin. "Suzanne, what's going on? Are you moving this?" Panic crossed her face as she stared at me. "Are you okay?"

I could barely get the words out. "It's Mary! It's Mary... Magdeline..." I stammered. "Oh my God, this is AMAZING!" For a moment I thought I was going to pass out from the sheer ecstasy of the experience. For surely, that blast between the ears I was getting had to be none other than Mary Magdeline herself.

If, in fact, such things were possible.

Then, just as suddenly, everything stopped. The planchette became still on the Ouija board as the tsunami of energy drained from my body. I was limp, exhausted. Empty.

Ming Yin and I looked at each other. I was speechless.

"What in God's name is going on in here?" asked Divina from the doorway.

"I think...I think Mary Magdeline just dropped in," I stammered. "Did you invite her?"

Divina crossed her arms. "Hmmph," was all she said.

We watched her walk away, then Ming Yin and I looked at each other.

Something undeniably huge had just happened. Uncomfortably, I shifted in my seat, unsure what this meant.

Perhaps I didn't want to know.

CHAPTER SEVEN

The lion finally had to lie down, mainly because there was nowhere else to go. The full freight of my losses had finally begun to sink in.

The night before I dreamed of my father in a scene that was entirely blue. He stood before me in a long, white robe. My father, who had been an artist in his lifetime, held up a small, framed painting.

It was of a holy temple in the snow. The painting was radiant, glowing with divine love. It was exquisitely beautiful, and yet it, too, was entirely blue. While the painting exuded spiritual grace, it was sad and lonely as well.

In the dream, my father held it out to me as if to say, *This is where you are now and it's okay. This, too, is a sacred place.*

I woke up that morning knowing that I was in my own personal Blue Period and that it would eventually end. Moreover, I could feel the privilege and the perfection of being in such a place, for alongside the pain was pure spiritual essence. My father had shown up to remind me.

My grief had finally arrived. I lay in bed, unable to move, or I dissolved into tears in strange places—while doing the laundry or taking a walk. A good deal of my grieving was a pronounced inability to do much of anything.

The rest of it was all about denying that I was grieving. Or believing that I was going to 'do grief better' and not fall apart like all those other mothers who'd lost their children.

Really, at the end of the day, my grief was like a temporary insanity.

It was as if a thick layer of cotton wool had been wrapped around my brain, and all my formerly sharp synapses were barely in motion. I found I couldn't make decisions. Nor could I follow the simplest of directions. I became easily confused and exhausted. A therapist later explained to me that a part of the brain is literally disabled by grief, allowing us to rest and process. So, all of this was, in fact, to be expected.

Helpful literature arrived in small packets from the organ donor agency, and I devoured it. Pamphlets reminded me that it was okay to feel completely lost, that no one was expecting me to be 'normal,' nor did I need to be. It encouraged me to talk about my grief with others or join a support group of other grieving parents, even to eat a pint of Ben & Jerry's if I needed to.

It also gently suggested if I wanted to kill myself, I should immediately seek help.

Meanwhile, I carried on alone. A kind woman named Karen from the organ donor agency would call now and then to make sure I was okay. "Let me know if you need anything," she'd say kindly.

"I'm fine," I'd say. "But I'm sure my former husband would love to hear from you," I'd add, attempting to be helpful.

Despite the fact that I could no longer escape my pain, I told myself I was still 'fine.' I still didn't need anybody's help. I could even work if I wanted to.

Or so I thought.

Day after day, Divina and Ming Yin went off to their jobs and there I was, blessedly alone with my grief. All I could do was lounge in bed, write essay after essay about my loss, and drink superfood smoothies.

But oh, how I longed to *do* things. For this is how I'd always dealt with crises—by getting busy. So, after a few months I attempted to launch the new business I was building when Teal died. I did this on the premise that I needed the money, despite the fact that I'd recently collected my divorce settlement. I had money in the bank that I could live on for quite a while if necessary.

Fifty game women registered for the initial teleseminar series, but by the end only a few remained. Teaching each class was like dragging myself through a field of broken glass. I could barely do it.

I shouldn't have been surprised. The night before the class began, I dreamed that I was in a burning building and alarms were blaring. I was caught in a fire that would destroy everything, and I had to run for my life.

When I woke, I could feel the message of the dream: a metaphorical fire was burning me alive, destroying literally everything about my previous life. I would only survive if I left the building quickly, taking nothing with me.

My friend Andrea had recently started coaching me on what was left of my business. More accurately, she kept telling me to stop. "You need to let go," became her mantra.

But still I hung on through those first winter months of my new life, unable to surrender my need to be busy, to be doing, to be frenetic. For I knew, once I stopped, the bottom really would drop out, utterly and completely.

I fought this place of inaction and scrambled to come up with something, anything to keep me busy. But finally, I began to slow down until I finally dissolved into days filled with nothing. My former business slipped away, unnoticed.

There was nothing left to replace it. Nothing, that is, but lots and lots of time. Now instead of working, I began compulsively signing up for hikes with a local chapter of the Sierra Club. Yet on the night before each hike, or perhaps on that very same morning, I'd find I couldn't get out of bed and I would cancel.

Or I would drive, drive, drive to some godforsaken trailhead, determined to attend, only to stop before I got there and turn around, unable to proceed.

Still, I clung fervently to the notion that everything was 'fine' and that I was 'fine' and that things were relatively normal. I honestly believed I could do this breakdown alone, that I didn't need any help. And so I drove.

It was on one of these drives that I met up with Teal again.

She showed up just five miles short of the trailhead, and at first I wasn't sure what was happening. A blaze of radiant, sparkling energy suddenly shimmered through my body as I drove back through the West County hills. An old disco song, "Shake Your Booty," happened to be playing on the car stereo hooked up to my iPod.

I slowed down. I knew this feeling. It was unmistakable. It was Teal. It had been months since I'd felt her around me.

"Honey?" I asked cautiously.

Suddenly, it was as if I'd been hit with a joy-filled two-by-four. A radiant blast of energy cycled up through my body, filling every molecule of my being with absolute, total, magnificent joy.

I pulled over and stopped the car.

"Teal?" I asked again, not quite believing what was happening.

Another swell of the radiant force field overtook my body. It was the extreme happiness hit that my daughter had now become. Only she was no longer my child, or so she told me in in no uncertain terms.

I'm not your daughter anymore and you are not my mother. Teal no longer exists, she said.

Okay. "So…who are you now?" I asked curiously.

I could feel her amusement at the question. The answer came shuffling down the line.

Call me T.E.F.K.A.T. The Energy Formerly Known as Teal.

I smiled. The answer was one-hundred percent Teal.

Slowly, I started to drive down the country road before me. Somehow that seemed important to do…to keep on driving.

Now "Shake Your Booty" began its thunka-thunka disco climax on the car stereo.

Shake shake
Shake shake
Shake shake
Awwwwwww
Shake shake

The happiness surge just kept on flowing and was now pulsing in time with the music. Tears of utter and complete joy began pouring down my face, none of which I could pin a reason on.

The joy and the tears simply were.

I attempted conversation. "So now you like disco?" I croaked in an attempt at otherworldly humor. Teal had always been into the blues when she was alive.

Instantly, I was filled with understanding that seemed to come from outside myself. The vibration in the music was a lure, a link, a connection—a place where my mind relaxed and my heart let go, allowing me to open up to the other side.

For me, apparently, disco was helpful. Which, in and of itself, blew my mind.

A chorus line of cartoon goblins now filled my head. They were tall and white, like characters from *Casper the Friendly Ghost,* a cartoon I watched as a child. Here were my spirit guides, line dancing in some divine reinterpretation of *Soul Train.* They appeared to be having a really good time.

"Seriously?" I asked aloud. Then a most amazing thing happened.

Another blast of joy cycled up through me, only this one

erupted into laughter. It was high-pitched, angelic, and it came sailing out of my mouth.

It was not my laugh.

I pulled over again. I was having trouble understanding what had just happened.

"Honey? Is that you?" I asked again. "Are you…laughing? Through me?"

The swirl of energy in my body spun centrifugally, spiraling up in an instant, and a bigger laugh erupted and continued. After a moment it quieted. It was nothing less than confirmation.

I still had no idea what I was laughing about, but it didn't matter. I surfed on an afternote of sweet, lingering bliss.

Briefly I thought I might be losing my mind, that my grief had pushed me to the edge of insanity. But then another instant wave of knowing settled through my body.

I had been given this gift along with the loss. I would be forever connected to Teal, and she would heal me…as much as I allowed. The healing would happen in my car, and in other places, too.

I had no words as I began to understand what was happening.

Instead, I slowly turned the car around, one more hike forsaken. I seriously needed to go home.

So, the car became my new meeting ground with Teal. I could see the perfection of this. I bought my car, a teal-blue Honda, when I was leaving San Francisco. At the time, Teal and I agreed to name it after the childhood nickname she'd outgrown —The Tealster.

We'd taken it for a ride up and down the hills of San Francisco that first day I owned it, cranking up the radio and laughing with joy. It was the sweetest of memories.

The car became my mobile altar to Teal. After her death, I had a vanity plate made up that said TEALSTR. I had a custom license plate holder made that quoted one of the many small, channeled phrases she'd recorded in her journal.

It said, *Give Fearlessly and You Shall Never Want.*

On the back window, I added a decal of one of the goddesses she loved, White Tara, seated tranquilly on a lotus flower. White Tara was known for her compassion, healing, and sensitivity, just like my daughter was. And on the glove box cover, I stuck a tiny framed picture of Teal herself. I scattered rose petals in the cup holders and fastened a small metal statue of Kwan Yin to the dashboard. It was a perfect representation of my spiritual-not-religious beliefs.

My car now became my connection point with Teal, or T.E.F.K.A.T., or God, or the Universe, or whatever this cosmic fireball was that came barreling through my heart and my body as I drove. But then…that was what altars were for, right?

Gone was all my doubt about the afterlife. It had evaporated right along with my business and my plans for the rest of my life.

My link to Teal would now happen through songs and laughter and long drives to nowhere—all, improbably, fueled by disco. My takeaway was that each time she appeared, I was uplifted, energized.

Healed.

Part of me knew that this was just the beginning.

CHAPTER EIGHT

I lay in the half-light of another empty dawn, barely awake. The word 'Gia' and an urn of ashes flashed across my mind. *Gia?*

I rolled on my back and contemplated this. *Gia who?* I reached for my phone and Googled 'Gia.' An hour later I was still reading.

Gia Carangi was a supermodel born only a few years after me. She grew up in a house on the other side of Philadelphia from my own childhood home. Like me she was a long-legged tomboy when she was young, and a secret lesbian who preferred not to be out. In my own life, I'd waited until age 52 to come out, but Gia never did.

Gia was also needy and manipulative, a drug addict, and breathtakingly beautiful. She cycled out of this life at age twenty-six, a heroin addict who'd contracted AIDS. She went from being one of the most sought-after supermodels in the world, appearing on the covers of *Vogue* and *Cosmopolitan,* to working in the cafeteria of a nursing home, completely broken by her addiction.

And now she was dead.

I looked out the window at the California sunshine and

considered my path. The matter of my addiction to my former partner, a woman I'd tried to leave unsuccessfully three times, swam up to the surface. Love addiction, they called it.

Each day as I lay in my bedroom, my grief over losing Teal was punctuated with white-hot flashes of anger directed at my former lover, Whit. Lately they'd been getting more and more intense.

It was as if I couldn't put our relationship aside and just let bygones be bygones, even though we no longer spoke or had anything to do with each other. Again and again, I played out every slight, every taunt, and every grievance she had against me, and I boiled with fury.

For the first time in my life, I wanted to seriously hurt another person. In fact, I wanted to physically destroy Whit. My rage was all I had left in the soul-sucking vacuum that had once been our relationship, and I was clinging to it for all I was worth.

Like an addict.

Like Gia.

I thought about the words that woke me up on a sunny morning just after Whit and I broke up. *Read about love addiction.*

And I flashed on my financial adviser's comment at a recent appointment. "Suzanne, you've got to stop spending and debting compulsively." It seemed I was addicted to debt as well.

At the time she asked me to pay off my $5,700 credit card debt. I could afford to pay off this bill, but somehow the mere idea frightened me, so I didn't. Strangely, I needed that debt, just like I needed Whit. And just like Gia needed those hits of heroin.

This need was as old and familiar as the hills. *Who would I be without it?*

Slowly, the light played across the ceiling above me, as I considered this question. My obsession with Whit was no different from my avoidance of my finances. Both were useful in escaping the true matter at hand—my deep, crushing grief at losing my daughter, my marriage. My career. The very structure of my life.

Then I remembered the promise I had made to myself as I sat beside Teal's dying body: I had to clean up my act and become a better person no matter what it took. And now was most certainly the time.

I would deal with my addictive behaviors and stop being so continuously zoned out. I would stop being such a frenetic workaholic and a bully. And I would become a kinder, more compassionate person like Teal was. This I would do in my daughter's memory.

So, my path became clear that sunny November morning. I was definitely going to need some help. A few days later, I found it in the basement of a church, in a room full of recovering love addicts.

"I'm a romance addict, I guess," said the blond, seated on the metal folding chair next to me. Like me, she was new to the group.

Black, white, skinny, fat, prostitutes, and college professors, it didn't matter. We were all the same. Every last one of us had a problem with our oversized, needy hearts.

"I'm Suzanne," I began uncertainly when it was my turn. I hesitated, unsure what to say, next. "I'm…uh…glad to be here," I finally concluded.

Of course, I wasn't glad to be there at all. I totally didn't want to be part of this club, and even held out the tiniest bit of hope that I wasn't actually a love addict. After all, I didn't read romance novels addictively like some women in the room, or compulsively pick up people in bars. Nor had I ever once cheated in any of my relationships.

I was merely obsessed with an unavailable woman to the point where I wanted to beat her up. I had simply fallen desperately in love with someone who needed to hurt and control me. That was *all* that was wrong, my injured mind insisted.

Did that really make me a love addict?

Well, okay, there was also that thing with Rita. But was that really addictive, just because I rushed into it weeks after breaking up with Whit? It felt so good to be with someone who was kind and loving after all the abuse I'd suffered. Even if I knew, deep in my heart, that it wasn't meant to be.

Was this really so addictive?

Not enough can be said for the power of denial.

As it turned out, the dynamic I'd played out with Whit was a textbook case of love addiction, a push-pull dynamic requiring both the 'obsessive grasper' and the 'love avoidant' who recoils in the face of true love.

In that first meeting with my fellow love addicts, I listened to the stories of the women around me and struggled to see where I fit in. Yet, at the same time, I knew exactly where I fit in. It was a truth I could barely tolerate.

Seated in my folding chair, I danced between deep recognition and wanting to run from the room as fast as I could.

Finally, near the end of the meeting, something shifted. It was the moment when newcomers were invited to speak, and since the only other newcomer had already left, all eyes now turned to me.

I squirmed in my seat. The silence ticked on as the others waited for me to speak.

I knew I needed to say something, but what? What pre-arranged words could I deliver that would make me palatable, appropriate to this group of strangers...and safe? The gears in my brain buzzed and clicked, trying to lock the algorithm into place.

How in God's name could I even talk about this?

As I sat there, my addictive behavior seemed so flawed and so beyond repair, it overwhelmed me completely. How could I ever stop running obsessively after difficult people like Whit— or, for that matter, lose myself in dalliances when dating was the last thing I should be doing?

For that matter, how on earth was I ever going to untangle the elaborate Gordian knot that my finances had become? Could I ever actually pay off my debt, and stop debting and compulsively spending altogether?

Even the simplest task, like closing a few of the seventeen bank accounts I had scattered between New York and California seemed completely overwhelming.

Yet, there was a larger question, too. How could I ever begin to get back to that tiny, frightened, vulnerable person I had once been so many years earlier? The true Suzanne—the one who kept my flame, the one Teal knew and loved when she was little —had somehow dried up and disappeared.

All that was left now was this brittle, angry, lost shell of a person. Somehow I knew that sitting in these meetings was the beginning of the repair.

Finally, I cleared my throat and spoke.

"I'm here because my daughter just died," I began. "And it may not seem like this has anything to do with addiction, but it has everything to do with it," I said. Then I began to cry.

I talked and they listened, and so the egg was broken. By the end of the meeting, I knew a remedy would be found. Somehow I was going to find my way back to peace.

In the meetings and the weeks that followed, I began to realize something: God always has a plan. Like…always.

For as much as I resisted, avoided, pretended and muddled, I could not get away from one single, sterling truth: my life was now in shambles and I had no choice but to become humble before God and my fellow addicts, tell the truth, and get on with my healing.

Soon I became a regular at these meetings. I also joined a group of recovering compulsive debtors and shoppers who, like me, had stayed vague about their money and so found themselves in all kinds of financial trouble.

As I sat on the folding chairs in an endless string of church basements, parish halls, and community centers, hour after hour,

I could feel my old shame flooding my body. I had always been too busy being perfect and beyond reproach to really take on my issues. But now I knew the truth.

You can't run from your own weaknesses. Sooner or later, they will overtake you, if you are lucky.

For only then can you truly begin to recover.

I lay in Teal's bed, her childhood belongings all around me. It was our first Christmas without her, and I'd come back to my former home to try and get through it with my son and my ex-husband. In fact, I'd chosen to sleep in Teal's room. It was still full of her essence.

Across from me was Teal's bookcase, which she'd carefully weeded through and reassembled in the month before her death. Instead of books, it now contained a brief history of her life.

On top were autographed photos of actors and singers she admired. There was also a large photograph of the two of us out on Lake Champlain, the 129-mile inland sea in front of the house. A small stack of beloved sweatshirts and hoodies filled the middle shelf, including a red one emblazoned with *Berklee College of Music,* the college she'd attended for two years.

On the bottom shelf were a pile of her shoes—blue cowboy boots from her blues period in Austin, and a completely broken-down pair of Keds that was full of holes. She'd worn these as she backpacked her way around parts of the world.

I sighed as I looked around her bedroom. Teal had been dead for four months, and still it seemed surreal. Impossible, really. I snapped off the light and lay down on the bed, attempting to go to sleep.

A few hours later, I finally gave up. I sat up and looked out the window over Lake Champlain. The blue night air was thick with snow and wind rattled the storm windows. It was just the sort of dramatic weather Teal would have loved.

I lay down and closed my eyes again, trying, yet again, to sleep. My mind relaxed and my body began to let go, and as it did, something shifted.

An awareness settled over me that I was not alone. I opened my eyes.

"Teal? Honey, is that you?"

The now-familiar warmth spread through my body, and then the surge of 1,000-watt joy. Teal was indeed here.

"So...what's up?" I asked, once again closing my eyes.

She was as terse as usual. *It's time to get this party started,* she said.

I stumbled over myself to stay in her thrall. "What party? What do you mean? Should I be doing something specific? You'll tell me, right?"

Silence ensued. I lay back on the pillow and waited, hoping something else would come. I was not disappointed.

For the next several moments, I had an experience that was completely transcendental. To this day, I'm not sure what happened exactly, though at the time it seemed to unfold most naturally.

It began quietly, with Teal's essence merging into mine in a way that was both profound and simple. It felt complete, as if our energies locked together completely, seamlessly aligned. My body and my heart felt full to bursting.

Suddenly a landscape opened up in my mind, and I could sense Teal in front of me, beckoning. My present reality disappeared at that point, and what filled my mind's eye was some kind of holographic dream.

We flew over...something...though words can hardly capture its iridescence and the depth of its overwhelming beauty. Call it an endless, shimmering lavender sea, or an ocean of dreams. All I know is that as we flew together, I could suddenly see all the limitations of my mortal life. I could see my resentments and my petty grievances, my foot-stamping demands, and my crushing fear.

The vast wellspring of pain, suffering and anxiety that binds us up every day of our lives became strikingly clear. The hugeness of it was startling.

Meanwhile, the lavender sea just kept unfolding beneath us, a shining path to perfect peace. We were disembodied, Teal and I. We were free and filled with magnificent joy, and we were flying, skimming right above the surface of the water. Together, we had become fairies or even angels.

In these few precious moments, we were lifted up together into some kind of celestial light that made us utterly buoyant with happiness. It was indescribably beautiful.

I knew this was my daughter's realm now, radiant, joyful, and free. A moment later I heard her parting words: *This is yours to share.*

As I became fully conscious, I felt light. Free. Uplifted.

And once again, I felt healed.

CHAPTER NINE

I woke up, and as was usual now, I began my day feeling lost. My mind kept replaying the various scenarios about how I could have saved Teal. If only I'd driven her home myself after dinner that night. Or I could have taken her to the Emergency Room, aware that she was acting strangely. Then she would have been in a hospital when she had her cardiac arrest. Someone could have revived her then, and she never would have suffered brain damage.

Instead, she'd be here today.

My perspective was bleak. I chided myself for having the wrong priorities, for not picking up the clues, for being so hopelessly self-involved. Bargaining, Elizabeth Kubler-Ross called it.

I opened up a blank Word document on my computer and let my thoughts pour out. And within only a moment or two, another voice occupied my head. It was Teal and she had a lot to say.

I typed as fast as I could, trying to get it all down.

I just died, and how is not important. Oh, Mom, your inquiring mind! Just let go and surrender to the inevitability of this. And no, you could not have prevented it. The time was important with the woman who drove me home 'cause I needed to affect her on a deep level, and everyone else as well. Even the shamans and the tribe who prayed for me.

Teal continued.

There is no accident here for this is a profound time of growth for you, Mom. And there is no mistake, for you are channeling all you can glean here for the people.

Her words settled over me like warm, melted honey. I considered what she was saying—that I was "channeling all I could glean here for the people." What did this mean, really? The prayers that followed her through those last tenuous six days of her life had, indeed, been deep. Even the tribal people of the remote village in the Ecuadorian jungle the lecturer spoke about that last night at dinner had heard of Teal's imminent death. And they prayed for her, as well.

She continued.

Just be in flow, Mom, and be in flow and be in flow. That is all any of us are meant to do, for our instruments are so finely guided and calibrated. I saw that when my body lost mine. What a gift it was to see it as I was lifting out to the other side.

I saw that I was small and afraid throughout my life, as so many we are here to help have been. That is your profound gift and mine—to do this healing.

The certainty of her message settled through me that day. I knew the truth of it. Just as I knew Teal, herself, in the moments just after her birth, when she was nothing more than a small bundle, laid in my arms. On that snowy day in a Greenwich Village hospital, I looked into her newly opened, teal-blue eyes and felt the surrender of deep recognition.

At such moments, an ageless understanding passes between us, a recognition of a shared path. Once again, we were forever bonded.

The aftermath of her birth was no less spectacular. The surgeon who performed the cesarean section gave me a time-released shot of morphine, a drug I was allergic to, as it turned out. So, for the next twenty-four hours, the floor of my room undulated, the artwork spun wildly on the walls, and nurses kept coming in to make sure I was still breathing.

While Teal was tucked safely away in the nursery, I was up all night, laughing, sobbing, having long, rambling conversations with the other new mother in the next bed. I was also reading the private pains and secret anguish of every single person who entered our room.

Suddenly I could see the roseate glow of their energetic fields and understand their deepest secrets. I saw what was aggravating them, where their hearts had been broken, and what was keeping them up at night. I could feel every ounce of their pain. And I found myself empathizing in ways I never had before.

The fact that I could suddenly do this was neither strange nor mystical. It simply was. And somehow, it had everything to do with Teal.

Finally, near dawn, a night nurse brought her into my room. "You can have her," she harrumphed. "She's a little devil!" Teal's voice was completely gone from crying all night, and her infant screams nothing more than scratchy rasps.

As I took her in my arms, she latched on to my breast immediately, and I looked up at the very annoyed nurse. Again, I could see her auric glow and read everything about her. Of course, she was grumpy, I thought to myself. She had a hell of a fight with her husband, and now she's had this wild, angry baby on her hands all night.

"Thank you," I heard myself say as I looked into the nurse's eyes. "I am so sorry for your troubles." The nurse softened slightly and she nodded. Then she slipped away.

Of course, I shouldn't have been surprised. This was only the beginning of Teal's deep and abiding influence on me. After a lifetime of being in push-push survival mode and feeling like I had to bludgeon life into cooperating with me all the time, suddenly I had glimpsed ease and kindness.

My daughter brought all of this into my life, even though at the time she was only nineteen inches long. But then that's how Teal rolled.

She was nothing less than the embodiment of love.

I drove through the streets of San Francisco, tunneling along my well-worn path back to the Golden Gate Bridge and my home up north. I'd just been to a pair of healers I knew just off Union Square. They were helping me cope, for now, six months after Teal's death. I was also grieving the death of my demented ninety-four-year-old mother.

Boo had passed away the previous week. Unlike Teal's death, hers had been anticipated. Even a blessing.

The city unfolded before me. In Chinatown, I turned on to Sacramento and climbed up, up, up, making my way north toward the Golden Gate Bridge. I was thinking about going home to a comforting plate of Trader Joe's frozen risotto when Teal dropped in. She urged me to head west instead, toward the sunset over the Pacific.

I could feel her warmth beaming through me once more. And almost involuntarily, a wide smile of joy spread across my face.

Still, I resisted her counsel. I just wanted to go home. But in my new effort to be all about surrender and going with the flow, I made a left and drove toward the beach. I couldn't say no to Teal and she knew it.

I crested a hilltop near Nob Hill, and the massive western sky spread out before me. With it came the great void, a lightness reflected in the sky that could only be the sea. The last licks of sunset were dying, and the city itself looked minor by comparison.

Only a half hour before, I had been lying on my friend Dave's massage table. Dave was a sunny surfer guy with a gift for spiritual healing. While working on my tense shoulders he kept up a running stream of commentary from my mother, now five days into the afterlife.

Again and again, Dave exclaimed, "I can't believe how much love I feel!"

The new version of my mother was not controlling, anxious or judgmental. Instead, she was nothing but warm, buttery love. And she was funny, as usual. Boo's edgy sense of irony was back and right there in the room with us. All the old barricades between us had magically evaporated.

So now, I drove along feeling the afterglow of my mother's love. The experience was a little surreal. I realized I needed to integrate this new lovable Mom, so different from the troubled alcoholic I'd known as a child.

I stopped at the light at the corner of Divisidero and Sacramento, and noticed how dark it was getting. Once again, I reconsidered a right turn toward home when Teal appeared once more. Her energy crackled through my body.

Would you just drive to the beach? she said in my head.

I hesitated.

You're going to ignore me now? she asked.

Okay, point taken, I thought. I hurtled forward into the darkening night. I was going to the sea, as requested.

All of my life as a mother I rushed my kids, my former husband, myself. We all marched to the urgent, commanding rhythm in my head—doing, striving, pushing, achieving. Teal had had enough of it by the time she died. Hence her silent request while she lay in a coma in the hospital: *Don't rush me, Mom.*

I wondered about this as I drove.

By the time I reached Ocean Beach, the sun had already set. Inky darkness filled the sky, and I could just make out a lone figure on the beach. It was a man, walking his dog. I sat there and thought back to the person I had been only six months earlier, back when I couldn't take the time to watch a sunset or sit in the dark in its aftermath. Now death had idled me, and I was no longer so driven.

In this moment, I was another person, making her way, doing her best to get along. Now I was like everyone else, even that guy walking his dog on the beach. And I was okay…just like this.

It occurred to me then that there might never be any 'bigger work' in this life of mine. Perhaps this self-improvement project *was* the bigger work. I realized then that I had nothing to prove. For once I could just relax and stop trying to force some kind of skewed perfection.

My mother, my harshest critic, was now dead. So, really, there was no one left to please.

No one, that is, except for me.

The psychic peered at me and blinked. Joanne was in a hotel room in London, and I was sitting on my bed in Petaluma. We were speaking on Skype.

"Who is Rose?" she asked. "Teal is telling me that Rose is important. She has something helpful for you."

Rose?

My mind drew a blank. "I don't know," I said vaguely.

"Keep an eye out for Rose," Joanne said.

Like me, this psychic had lost a child many years earlier. She was part of a new sisterhood of grieving mothers I now found myself in. The reading was a gift from Nicky, another bereaved English mother in our tribe who had quickly become a dear friend.

"Teal is around you all the time," Joanne continued. "That flickering kitchen light…the one above the sink. That's Teal."

I paused. We did have a kitchen light that flickered sometimes. And it was right above the sink.

"Also, you're going to feel like you have to have a pen all the time, Suzanne," Joanne continued. "You'll be writing constantly. Next year you will make money again as a writer. Teal is confirming this with the gift of a comforter."

Joanne hesitated. "You'll maybe…give someone a quilt? That's how you'll know you are on the right track with your work."

Tears sprang into my eyes. I had indeed given Teal's comforter to Ming Yin, my housemate, because she often complained of being cold. She had told me how she thought of Teal sometimes at night, when she was snuggled down under her quilt.

I sighed. Everything Joanne said was not only accurate, it was carved deep in my soul. Here was at least the beginnings of the roadmap I'd been searching for.

"And another thing," Joanne continued as she neared the end of the reading. "You'll know Teal is around you when the song "Dancing Queen" comes on over the car stereo and you start dancing in your car. This is just more confirmation, love."

While "Dancing Queen" hadn't popped up on my car stereo yet, I was most certainly dancing. Tuning in to the zap of Teal's energy as I drove was a daily highlight, and it was always fueled with dance-appropriate songs on the iPod.

I clung to these few precious moments of ecstatic, life-giving joy for all I was worth. They were my lifeline, my anchor, and oddly, the only thing that seemed real in my life at that moment.

A week later, Joanne's words proved correct.

I had gone to my beloved hot springs, a place called Harbin north of the Bay Area. Here, magical things happened. Naked people lazed in the warm pool under a huge fig tree, ripe with figs, as they watched the stars overhead. We sat silently in the pools here, somehow all of us intrinsically connected.

It was here that I ran into a friend, a woman whose name I always forgot. "Suzanne," she began as she stroked my arm consolingly. "I read about Teal on Facebook. I'm so sorry."

I closed my eyes to ward off the ever-present swell of tears. "Thank you," I murmured.

"I have something to recommend," she said. "Have you read Anita Morjani's book, *Dying to Be Me*? It might be helpful."

Something shifted in my psyche. She had a book for me. *It might be helpful,* she said.

I looked at my friend's face and her name came swimming back to my mind.

It was Rose.

I smiled. "If you recommend it, I will read it," I said.

We hugged. Then I happened to look down on the ground. There on the driveway gravel between us was a guitar pick. It was just the kind Teal often used.

I picked it up and put it in my pocket and, as I did, a shiver of confirmation ran down my spine.

God was, indeed, good.

And, as if on cue, "*Dancing Queen*" started playing on the car radio as I drove home from Harbin the next day. This time, I car danced with abandon.

I walked up the stairs of feeling elated. It was close to 10 PM and I had just successfully booked travel for something I'd dreamed of doing for at least thirty years: spending two months in Paris.

Things felt right in my heart—even though I had no idea where I would stay in Paris, nor did I know how it would be to work there. Would I feel comfortable and grounded enough to write?

And did it even matter if I did? It had been nearly a year since I'd actually earned a living.

My mother would have wanted me to do this, I reasoned, for Paris was a place we'd traveled to once when I was younger. It was a place we'd both loved. In her will, she'd left me just enough money to go, if I spent it very carefully.

My soul was singing and happy as I settled under the covers. As it happened, I was back in Teal's old childhood bedroom, where I'd joined Luke and Larry on the first anniversary of her death.

I opened up Facebook for an end-of-day scan and saw a message from Kate, a fellow writer whom I'd recently heard about from a friend. Kate said she'd just had an unexpected seizure while visiting friends who lived on Teal Lane. She was hoping we could talk.

Naturally I was interested. I clicked on Kate's page and began to read her post about the benign brain tumor that had caused her seizure. Suddenly a message box popped up, and I saw that Kate was messaging me.

Can you talk now? she asked.

Within a few moments we were on the phone, and an other-worldly calm descended the moment our conversation began.

As Kate told me about her seizure, something shifted for me. My listening became soft and gentle, and I melted into the phone. Spirit, or perhaps TEFKAT, had overtaken me.

"It all began with the death of my spiritual mentor," Kate began. She talked of listening to this mentor in a dream just as her seizure began. Her mentor said to her: "The veil to the other side is thinner than you think."

Involuntarily, the TEFKAT laughter rippled through my body as she said this. Light, angelic, surreal. It laughed again as Kate described the intense, yet fully awake experience of her seizure.

At that moment, a shroud of fast, high energy whooshed through me, a tingling bed of flames that began in my heart and spread through my body. I surrendered just a bit more to the feeling.

Now I began to talk in a radically softened voice that flowed through me. It didn't seem to be me that was speaking, but some other energy that had borrowed my mouth.

"You and I are receptors, Kate," I heard myself say. "We have been brought together to inspire each other."

In that instant, I could see everything. The reason for Teal's death. The purpose of the path I was on. Even why I needed to go to Paris. Both Kate and I were being prepared for expansion beyond our wildest dreams.

And we were being brought together now in some kind of shared reckoning.

I felt completely connected to Kate. Our souls were touching as deeply as if we had fallen in love, or given birth to one another, or witnessed each other's deaths.

And yet there was a lightness, here, too—a detachment. So, if Kate and I never spoke again that would be fine, too. Understanding flooded my body and I could see the tender link between being Teal's mother and mothering the planet in just the way I am meant to do.

Suddenly, in this conversation with a relative stranger, I understood that for the remainder of my life I would travel to and fro between worlds, like a mystic. Like a shaman.

Like a receptor.

In biochemistry, this is the molecule that convey signals within a cell from the exterior—the other side, so to speak. Now I understood why Teal looked at me the way she did that last night in the restaurant as we listened to a speaker explain how shamans traveled between two worlds.

Her eyes were so full of wonder then, lit with an understanding I couldn't grasp. Her expression said, *Pay attention, Mom. You'll be needing this.* And now her message was clear.

That night at dinner, Teal was already on her path to the other side, and she was inviting me to come along. To be a shaman…her shaman. To bring forth divine energy, as well as her energy, just as it was needed.

Now it all made perfect sense.

Moments later, I hung up, awash with gratitude and forever changed.

I sat down on the bed and looked around the strange new room. A large red rose was painted across one of the walls, and an empty cupboard stood waiting for my clothing. Behind the big brass bed was a window covered with sheer white curtains.

Beyond that was Paris.

As if on cue, an emergency vehicle rushed by as its distinctive two-tone siren filled the room. I pulled back the curtains and looked out over a sea of mansard rooftops. Here it was: magnificent, gray Paris in all her elegance. I'd made it. Nonetheless, a huge wave of grief managed to find me in that moment. I sat down on the bed and began to sob.

What was I thinking, coming halfway across the world in the midst of my grief? I knew almost no one here. I was going to have to navigate a foreign city, calculate the currency, and somehow speak a language I was hardly fluent in. Even the recovery meetings were entirely in French.

I would be here for two months. *What the hell was I doing?*

At that moment, my new housemate knocked on the door. I'll call her Anya. "Are you ready?" she asked. I sighed. Anya had insisted we go to dinner as soon as I arrived. It was a get-acquainted meal intended to help us bond.

"Be right there," I called, blowing my nose and trying to pull my act together. I'd been awake at this point for nearly twenty-four hours, unable to sleep on the flight from San Francisco. Furthermore, my luggage hadn't made it. All I had presently were the clothes on my back.

I was shaky. Very shaky. For another thing, I could already tell Anya was going to be a problem. I could feel it the minute I walked into the apartment. Nothing unsettling had been said, still the tension in the place was palpable.

Anya was an acquaintance of a friend of mine who lived in Paris. After he told her about my situation, she invited me to stay with her and offered me the incredible rate of $35 a night for my room, purely out of the kindness of her heart. How could I refuse?

But now the reality of sharing two months in the apartment of a potentially unstable person began to sink in. Half an hour later I sat across from her, eating tandoori and hoping for the best.

Anya soon began a litany of complaints about her miserable existence, much of which had to do with her long, protracted divorce and her inability to get a job in France. As a Polish expat, there were complicated visa issues, she said. Her life here in the well-heeled fifth arrondissement was very, very hard indeed.

On and on she went in an endless monologue of anger, anxiety, and negativity. As she did, I could feel my inner five-year-old scrambling for safety. Anya had completely triggered all of my oldest, darkest, muddiest shit.

At first, I tried to be helpful, offering a string of suggestions, all of which were quickly rebuffed. This triggered a cascade of anger which I did my best to repress. I felt like I was back with my alcoholic, suicidal mother, who had steadfastly ignored all of my helpful codependent advice throughout my childhood.

I could feel myself getting huffier and huffier as I sat there. Finally, I gave up and just let Anya spew.

She concluded the meal by reminding me how kind she was to offer me such a reasonable rate for her room. "I did it for you out of compassion for your tragedy," she announced. "You'd never get a room even close to this price anywhere else in Paris." I thanked her. Yet again.

Then she regarded me warily. "Suzanne," she asked, "why did you come to Paris, anyway?"

God only knew, I thought to myself bleakly.

"Because I need to be here to heal," I replied. "Practicing my

70

French again and being in a place that I love will be good for me. Anyway, it seems like fun to make friends with some Parisians," I added as an afterthought.

Anya laughed darkly. "Well, *that* will never happen!" she declared. Then she leaned toward me and lowered her voice. "Parisians don't befriend visitors. Not unless they want to have sex with you. I can guarantee you right now you will never be invited to anyone's house for dinner, unless they want to seduce you. I never have, and I've been in Paris for ten years."

Later, I lay in bed and wondered at my situation. How in God's name was I going to live with this woman? I closed my eyes and asked for help. *Show me what to do*, I prayed.

As if on cue, guidance arrived. I was filled with a sudden awareness that there was only one right thing to do. I had to love this woman unconditionally.

I didn't need to fix her, or heal her, or even like her. I just needed to let her be the way she was and go about my business. I knew I couldn't change her, nor was it my job to. Nor was I to attempt to please her or even help her solve her problems.

Instead, just give her kindness, my inner voice urged. *That is all that is ever required.*

Immediately, I felt humbled. Apparently, this was a test of my compassion and my inner strength.

But I should have known. This was exactly what Teal would have done.

Given how triggered I was by Anya, the task at hand was going to be damn near impossible, that was for sure.

I sat down on the park bench in the Place de Vosges and looked around.

Red-striped masonry buildings rose all around me in beautiful order, and a fountain splashed pleasantly in front of me.

Once Teal and I had walked through this park together. It was the oldest square in Paris, and it was rife with ghosts.

I missed her something fierce that day, but as usual she was never far away. In fact, she seemed to be everywhere. When I opened Facebook that morning, the first thing I saw was a picture from two years earlier: Teal eating a chocolate croissant in a park near the Eiffel Tower.

I closed my eyes and remembered Teal's half-smile as I took her picture by the fountain that day. She'd been working on a farm in Belgium at the time and had come to Paris to join me for the weekend.

I had delivered a critical package of anti-seizure meds to Teal, one of which was a new generic she'd never tried before. Yet, as we passed through the Place des Vosges, the new medication was having a strange effect on her. She was irritable, depressed, and unsettled.

We stopped for a café down the street, and Teal barely looked at me the entire time. "I'm sorry," she finally said. "It's these meds, Mom. They're screwed up." Then she burst into tears. "I'm really sorry," she said sadly, shaking her head. "I just…"

She couldn't finish her sentence. I looked at my daughter and felt utterly helpless. I couldn't even imagine what she was going through.

Now I sat with my memories on a bench in the Place des Vosges and fought back the urge to weep in public. I got up and began to walk.

Moments later I crossed the Seine on the Quai Louis Philippe, heading for Notre Dame's massive medieval towers that rose above the fall trees. Like the beacon that it always has been, the cathedral beckoned me, and I followed. I joined the long line of people in front and patiently waited to go inside.

Twenty minutes later, I walked into Notre Dame's vast, soaring stillness. Ancient air loomed above me, and all around me hung a monumental gloom. I found my way to the nave.

There was no service in progress at the time. Here and there, people sat in contemplation. Silently I walked up the side aisle, and as I did a pristine chorus of young women's voices suddenly filled the cathedral. There were probably about twenty of them, a choir of high school girls not unlike my daughter had once been.

They were nothing less than angelic.

Slowly, I walked toward the music. I could feel the pure, sweet, spiritual ecstasy that has made Notre Dame so beloved for centuries pour through me.

I'm not a religious person, but if I were this might be one of those moments of divine transcendence. For when I got to the transept the girls began singing the familiar opening bars of my favorite piece of music, Mozart's "Ave Verum Corpus." The beautiful interweaving of sunlit voices and the soaring piano line poured through the air. I stood stock still, letting its grace fill my heart.

I knew something then: I would get through this. In fact, I already had to some degree. I was here, and I was soundly committed to my healing. That was all that was required now.

The message was clear. I really could relax and trust God.

———

I woke up in the half-light of a weekday morning and, blinking, looked around my bedroom, remembering where I was. Immediately, I felt the great spiritual swirl all around me.

Moments earlier I had been deeply lost in a dream. I'd found my way into a cooperative community of advanced souls. They shared coffee mugs collectively in their kitchen, each mug bearing the symbol of what its owner brought to the group. There were words like 'abundance' and 'generosity' written on the mugs.

Yet I walked into this kitchen willfully, and just took a mug off the shelf without understanding whose it was, or even reading the carefully written rules on the wall. After all, I wanted my coffee.

Did it seriously matter which mug I used?

In the dream this mattered very much, which was explained to me by a kind but firm spirit guide. Suddenly I stopped, looked around at the others in the room and felt intensely vulnerable and afraid.

The spirit guide then showed me that this was where earthly bodies could retrieve, heal, and resolve old soul memories—even those memories that caused you to fear other people.

At that moment, I woke up. As I lay there, I heard my guide speak to me directly.

You are being taught living compassion, it said.

I asked who was speaking to me.

Source, came the reply.

Suddenly I understood the crushing fear of people that had consumed me all of my life. It was an open wound that could not be touched. Over it I had placed the Band-Aid of my arrogance, my greed, my ambition. And my unkindness.

I thought about the intense vulnerability I felt in the dream —even in the company of kindly, advanced souls. Perhaps compassion really was the way back to happiness for me.

I moved through my day after that dream knowing something had shifted for me, ever so slightly.

I was getting better.

CHAPTER TEN

The dream was just a fragment, but it was a powerful one. I woke up in a little more amazement than usual.

Teal appeared with seriously Botoxed lips and dreadlocks dyed in wild shades of purple and green. A plastic surgeon had carved her face so that she looked like a parody of a TV star. Topping off the look was a pair of impenetrable mirror sunglasses.

I knew this was an elaborate disguise that she was putting on to teach me something about myself. Then Teal spoke to me directly. *They're telling me… 'Unmute your phone,'* she said. 'They' were my spirit guides.

Pulling out the notebook beside my bed, I scribbled down the dream, just as I had done with each dream I'd had over the last year and a half. Then I sat back and considered this latest message. My actual cell phone had, in fact, been on mute ever since Teal's death. I'd turned off the ringer because I hadn't been able to tolerate any kind of intrusion.

But now this dream had a much larger meaning. 'Unmute your phone' had something to do with being open to receive God's guidance. That much was clear.

Perhaps the storm was beginning to pass, and once again I

could open up to life completely. A written stream of consciousness followed, and the guidance was terse this time.

Stop turning down your megaphone. Put it out there, Suzanne. Be as loud as want. Do not hold back. Do not hesitate to be your full, forceful personality.

Yet again, I was being urged to be myself. To stand in my true power, my vulnerability, without the old egoic cloak of self-righteousness. I didn't have to prove myself to anyone anymore, nor did I have to be a flashy, impressive, attention-getting 'star.'

That false persona I'd cooked up so many decades ago was a way of holding myself back from others. It was a way of staying safe. And yet, that old childish defense was from a time when people around me seemed dangerous and expectations ran high. My world had completely changed since then.

Ironically, despite all I had been through, life had become truly safe again, mainly because I was learning how to take care of myself.

Now I could just be me. I could be loud, messy Suzanne, as flawed as I needed to be. It was safe to be seen. And it was safe to unmute my phone and let the world connect with me once more.

So, the next right thing to do presented itself. As ever, it was to walk through the streets of Paris. For it was here, each day, I was finding just a little more strength and courage.

That day I went on a walk to Rue Montorgueil, a street Monet had once painted in an ecstatic, flag-waving blur. This ancient, cobbled street allowed no cars. Instead, it was packed with happy, relaxed people doing two things—buying groceries from Paris's gorgeous cheese mongers, butchers, and bakeries that lined the street, and socializing in its cafés.

As I wandered among the jean-clad Parisians and the backpack-wearing tourists in the Sunday sun, all was right with the world. All of us were connected by the simple act of buying groceries and taking a moment to relax.

The purchase of a small square of Comte cheese, along with

some bread and a few good pates, put me back together that morning. And as I sat at a sidewalk café on the Rue Montorgueil drinking a café noisette and watching the passing crowd, once again I felt I was a part of the world.

My life could, and would, return to normal, one tiny step at a time.

———

Anya and I sat at the small round table by the kitchen window. Outside a clothesline of bras and panties waved in the breeze over the Rue de Turenne. Four weeks had passed since I'd moved in, and by now Anya was charging me for every last thing she could think of, including the use of her salt and pepper.

"How are you today, Suzanne?" she asked with a sneer. "And don't tell me you're *happy*, for God's sake! I don't want to hear it."

I said nothing, and we continued eating our breakfast in silence.

This appeared to be some kind of punishment for the fact that I was indeed happy and making friends with the French. Only the night before I'd gone to an incredible dinner party in the 1st arrondissement where the guests included a well-known motivational speaker from the UK, a popular French TV anchorwoman, a wine entrepreneur from Texas and her dashing French husband who looked like a cross between James Bond and Maurice Chevalier.

It was after 11 PM when dessert was served along with a fine bottle of French champagne. Our host presented the bottle and poured a glass for each guest. Then he flung open the doors to a small balcony beside the dinner table. There, framed in the doorway, was a breathtaking full moon. It was huge and luminous. "To beauty," our host said as he raised his glass. "Santé."

But by now I wasn't sharing such details with Anya. I knew

she wouldn't want to hear them. Instead, I kept a running litany of kindness mantras going through my head.

Anya is your host, and you are her guest.

Her pain is not your fault, and you don't have to fix it.

And finally, the kicker: *What would Teal do?* The answer was immediate.

Teal would be kind and compassionate. Teal would exude love. Teal would give Anya plenty of space. And mostly, Teal would not judge anyone for being different from her. Instead, she would be grateful to be there.

As for me, I was less of a saint. But rather than lash out at Anya, which I was incredibly close to doing most of the time, I made a habit of avoiding her.

In the odd moments that I actually spent with Anya, I managed to be civil. But just barely. That morning, however, something shifted. Anya sat across from me, solemnly eating her breakfast. I studied her for a moment and I could see all the pain that was etched on her tired face. She was far too young to look as old as she did, and I felt a sudden and unexpected wave of empathy.

"Anya," I said. She looked at me and frowned.

"You've been so generous to me, and I'd like to take you to dinner. To thank you." I ventured. "Tonight perhaps?"

Her look shifted to one of mild shock. "Oh," she said, regrouping. "I…uh…I'll have to let you know." Then she got up and left the room.

Within an hour, Anya had accepted my invitation. We went to dinner that night in a small restaurant that was a personal favorite of mine near San Sulpice called Le P'tit Fernand. Anya didn't know the place, but before she agreed to go, she researched it thoroughly. Then she decided to trust me. By that afternoon, she'd perked up considerably.

I hadn't seen Anya go out to a nice dinner, or even get dressed up in the month we had lived together, presumably because she couldn't afford it. So, by the time we got into the cab, she was genuinely excited. She'd spent time on her clothing and her make up, and she looked quite lovely that night. The worry was gone from her face, and all the way over to the restaurant, we chatted happily.

As we walked into the tiny, very classic French restaurant, Anya took in the scene and I could tell she approved of my choice. We ordered a good bottle of wine and got right down to business, inspecting the chalkboard menu.

Over coddled egg with truffles and *fois gras*, Anya told me about growing up poor in Poland, and how she'd made her way through university and an advanced business degree entirely on her own.

By the time our dinner arrived, I was sharing my own stories about growing up in a creative household with an artist father and a writer mother, which she found to be very exotic. We sailed through a fine dinner of *duck au cerise* for Anya and the sweetbreads in mustard cream sauce for me.

Suddenly a look of concern passed over Anya's face. "Do you think I'm going to be all right?" she asked.

In that moment, I could see Anya for who she really was. Against all odds, she had bootstrapped her way through life, but had yet to overcome her most basic fear. In fact, Anya was just like me. She, too, was struggling with the biggest obstacles she had ever known.

My heart opened easily, and in one sweep I forgave her for the many small transgressions I'd been tracking meticulously since I'd arrived.

"Of course you will," I told her. "You're going to be fine."

"Really?" she asked. "How do you know?"

Now all I wanted was to reassure Anya. A phrase from my recovery work ran through my mind: *principles before personalities.* It reminded me to let people have their personalities and, instead, to focus on my own core values and guiding principles. In that moment, I decided to forgive Anya for all of her pain and her rough edges.

I shrugged. "Look, Anya, all I know is that ultimately the world is good and people are kind. Anyway, we're still here, right?" I smiled and gestured at the scene around us. "I mean this ain't bad for two women who've lost pretty much everything."

She chuckled. Then I chuckled. Then we both laughed. We were just two fellow travelers who had chosen to walk the road together for a while. Then we toasted and we drank, because we were in France and that is what you do.

Then, of course, we ordered dessert.

As it turned out, my cocoon of benevolence with my house-mate Anya did not last. A week or so later, I was working in a café when my phone buzzed. Anya had sent me a text.

I need to speak to you immediately. Come home.

I looked at my phone. I wasn't planning to go home for hours, but an old familiar fear burbled up. It was the impulse toward self-defense that I'd known since childhood. Agree. Accept. Then disappear. No matter how bad the abuse is, just take it.

Do whatever it takes to be safe.

This was the same flawed logic that had propelled me through a number of difficult relationships. It was life without boundaries, and I was immensely tired of.

Anya's text was now followed by a call from her that I did not answer. Instead, I remembered the dream I'd woken up to that morning.

In the dream, I opened a text that said, *You need to start setting boundaries now.*

I looked around the café and sighed. I had no idea what Anya had on her mind, but I knew then that it was time to move on. I was simply no longer willing to be harassed by someone else's bad moods. Or pay for the use of the salt and pepper.

I opened up Craig's List and began looking for another space to stay. Within moments I was on the phone with a friendly

Australian, a cabaret singer named Mary. That morning, I rented a sweet little room in her apartment on the outer edges of Paris. Then I went home to tell Anya the news.

She met me at the door with a pronouncement. "You have forty-eight hours to move out, Suzanne," Anya began. "I simply can't tolerate having you here any longer."

"Actually, I'll be gone in an hour," I replied with a smile, as I headed off to pack my suitcases.

As I left, Anya stood by the door. I handed her my keys, then I leaned over to hug her but she couldn't quite manage that. "Goodbye, Suzanne," she said tensely. "We will not speak again."

"As you wish," I said.

Not surprisingly, Anya called twenty minutes later. "Are you going to retaliate?" she demanded into the phone.

"What?" I was dumbfounded.

"Because you left so quickly. You must want to retaliate."

I shook my head and I chuckled. "No, Anya, I won't retaliate." I paused. "If anything, I wish you well," I said, and I honestly meant it. An image of Anya came swimming to mind from the night we had dinner—the small, injured girl, whose hope, fear and vulnerability were so very transparent.

"I truly hope everything works out for you," I told her. "Anyway, I know you're going to be fine. Just hang in there and keep the faith."

Anya mumbled a goodbye, and as we hung up I finally understood that her pain was not my problem. Nor had Whit's pain been my problem, or my former husband's, my mother's, or anyone else's. None of it had ever been mine to resolve.

Furthermore, I didn't need to take their jabs personally. Instead, I could forgive these people just as I could forgive everyone who'd ever bothered me.

The truth was starkly clear. One way or another, we are all wounded creatures. Our job is simply to walk the path back to peace, one shaky step at a time. Some of us even have to make that walk on our knees, crawling toward self-forgiveness. I'd already learned that lesson firsthand.

Perhaps this was why I'd really come to Paris—to accept, to forgive, and to let go.

Now it was time to move on.

CHAPTER ELEVEN

I pulled the small sculpture of Ganesh, the Hindu elephant God, from its packing material and placed it carefully on my new altar. "The elephant statue," was how Joanne, the English psychic, had described it when she saw it in her reading. "Keep it near you when you are writing," she'd advised.

Ganesh is not only the remover of all obstacles; he is the patron of arts, letters, and wisdom—the writer's god—and his figure had been with me ever since I left Whit. It was time to begin writing the book I had been called to write, though I had no idea yet how it would end.

Outside the sliding glass doors in my new bedroom was a deck. Beyond it, the sun rose over a broad swamp that had recently filled with rain. I watched as several white geese glided onto the waters of this pop-up pond and floated by serenely. The sight immediately calmed me.

Everything had changed since I returned from Paris. I knew that going back to Divina's house in suburban Petaluma would be a mistake. Now I needed the peace, emptiness, and far deeper serenity of the countryside. I was ready for the next level of my healing.

I called my old friend Linda. "Move in with me," she said.

Linda, like me, was a veteran in Internet Marketing. We'd met years earlier at a conference when we had booths next to each other. We had celebrated many successes together. But we also propped each other up again and again in the worst of times.

Linda lived in a small, comfortable house at the edge of Sebastopol, an eclectic little town to the north. Like the rest of the West County, Sebastopol was chill, with a distinctly hippie vibe.

On an average day, you might run into a dog and its owner festooned in colorful, matching rags, both taking a nap in the sun outside of the town's tiny Whole Foods, apparently one of the first in the country. Or you might come upon a lone protester furiously marching along Main Street with a sign that says, *Bust Big Oil. No Pipeline!* as passing cars honk their approval. It was a place where on any given night you had your choice of Universal Dances of Peace, Vedantic chanting, or a performance by the local Love Choir.

Sebastopol is the kind of town where anyone, no matter how angry, broken, or just plain odd, could fit right in without being judged. On my second morning there, a man my age tapped me on the arm as I stood on a corner, waiting for the stoplight to change.

"I'm so glad you are here," he said, beaming at me. *Did I know this guy?*

He was a total stranger I'd never seen before.

He then handed me a small, golden card filled with single-spaced type. *Our every moment bliss is determined by how we bring our love & joy presents to every NOW moment...* the card began.

I thanked him, smiled back, and moved on. Then I tucked the card into my pocket, intending to put it on my altar. All around me, people were already doing their best to help me heal.

I got that now.

Since Teal's death I had come a long way. I'd allowed myself to stop working and simply rest. I read countless self-help books as I repaired my broken psyche. I joined a group for grieving parents. And I went to meeting after meeting with my fellow recovering addicts, and carefully did the work those programs required not once but multiple times.

I pondered, journaled, grieved and cried. I apologized and forgave. And I wrote my way through the worst of my pain. And somehow, in doing all of this, my need to be Superwoman began to evaporate. Now I understood that I was in the grip of a far bigger plan...one that required I become small and humble again.

I hadn't worked for more than a year, and by now I was living on one tenth of my former income. Yet, somehow, at the same time, my life felt deeply abundant. This was still more money than Teal had in her last year on Earth. Yet, when I offered her money, she refused it. "No thanks," she said graciously. "I have enough."

As ever, Teal modeled being in step with the Universe, needing little and appreciating what she had. Now I began to get it.

So instead of paying Linda rent, I cooked for her and took care of her dog when she left town. I read books from the library and bought my clothing at consignment stores, which turned out to be fun and interesting treasure troves. I swam in Sebastopol's beautiful public pool, the sun warming me all winter long. And I walked the brown, undulating hills and the muddy trails of the local parks, making my way along the black-berry brambles.

Then each day I settled down in my favorite tea shop in the center of town, bought a small pot of chai, and wrote. My work was simpler now. There was no longer anyone to impress or cajole with my writing. I no longer needed to sell anything or appear to be wise and profound.

Instead, I could just be...me.

It felt so good to be raw and real. People had responded in kind as I shared my blogs on Facebook. In turn, they told their own stories and voiced their encouragement. I felt far more intimately connected to my readers with each day that passed. But mostly, I felt more connected to myself.

One of the first mornings in my new bedroom, I woke up from a dream. Pre-dawn stillness surrounded me, and I began to cry. An image was seared into my brain, and I could not forget it.

In the dream, I made my way down a long, darkened corridor of locked doors. As I tried to open each one, I grew increasingly frustrated and anxious. Somewhere there had to be a place for me, but where was it?

The last door on the left suddenly opened, and as it did I walked into a beautiful, light-filled room awash with sunshine. I looked around me as an immense wave of relief poured through my body. This was where I was supposed to be.

At the edge of the room, I noticed another door and I tried it. This one also opened on to an even bigger, sunnier room. I stood in the doorway observing it, knowing that I would soon occupy this room, but not quite yet.

I closed my eyes and wept with pure gratitude.

Not long after that, I awoke to a vision.

Teal was holding out the deck of her beloved Goddess cards. She looked at me patiently, waiting for me to select one.

I pulled out a card and turned it over. It said *Marriage.*

She smiled at me and then she disappeared.

My new dating coaches, Ruth and Max, began by teaching me how to pray.

Now successful dating was no longer about wearing the right perfume and manipulating your way from one rendezvous to the next. Instead, my coaches were a pair of Bay Area PhD's, one of whom was a Buddhist/Christian teacher and the other a practicing shaman. They were also a happily married queer couple who'd learned a thing or two about love along the way.

Hiring them was part of my new structure for self-care, which included lots and lots of support. Even when it came to dating, I knew I couldn't do this alone.

"Say the Metta Prayer aloud when you meditate," Max suggested in a low, gentle voice.

Now I sat cross-legged on my bed, a pillow under my hips, intent on practicing. Across from me, candles flickered across my altar. Kwan Yin and Ganesh had the place of honor in the middle. A *Dia de los Muertos* scull festooned with a scarf and a curler sat beside a candle for Our Lady of Guadalupe, alongside a small laughing Buddha and a bell once given to me by a shaman.

Scattered here and there were rocks, shells, sand dollars and rose petals. Large photographs of my father, my mother, Teal and Luke were arranged against on the altar. A much loved, tiny picture of myself and my siblings when we were children nestled in tight to Kwan Yin, honoring my past and all that had brought me to this point.

These were my people, the people I loved, both living and dead. Along with each photograph was a memento or two: my father's tiny sketchbook, my mother's pearls and her scarf, a small watercolor Luke had painted, a lock of Teal's hair in a small basket. Each held some of their energy, a paean to the eternity we shared.

I closed my eyes and began to breathe slowly and rhythmically, my central nervous system letting go a little more with each long exhale. I held no thoughts in my mind. Emptiness took over and held me with love.

My mind would attempt to dart here and there, and sometimes a tangle of thoughts, ideas, and to-do's came barging in.

My practice was just to keep lovingly steering myself back toward nothing…to that pure, peaceful place of emptiness.

After a while, I began speaking the Metta Prayer aloud. It felt strange and awkward at first.

"May I be happy. May I know my true worth…" I began. My words sounded especially loud in the silent room, and tears unexpectedly filled my eyes. "May I know I am lovable," I croaked.

I stopped as tears ran down my face and sobbing overtook me. This was far more difficult than I thought it would be. Max had told me to repeat the prayer steadily for ten minutes, but I had only just started. How in God's name was I going to get through this?

"May I love and be loved with ease," I finally managed to say. I sighed the long sigh of a person dealing with something. Here it was, my own resistance to the very heart of my being.

I inhaled and repeated the prayer again, this time with a bit more ease. *May I be happy. May I know my true worth…*

Still, I wondered. Would I ever really know my true worth?

A parade of images from my past flickered through me. The loneliness of playing with my rusted metal dollhouse alone under the huge pine trees on our farm. Going home a sad failure after another day of being harassed by the kids at school. Lying at the bottom of the stairs, pretending I'd fallen down them so my distracted mother might finally pay attention to me.

But there were the triumphs, too. The unexpected poetry award, and the joy of rambling down the main street of our town as a teenager, visiting all the shopkeepers one by one. Arriving for my first day at college, and my first job in New York. Flying into London, Paris, Rome. The thrill of publishing my first book, my first article. Marrying Larry. Giving birth.

I had done so very much in my life, things others had not been able to do. Things I had taken for granted or dismissed as not very significant at all. And I had worked so very, very hard. This was a truth I could barely touch.

I continued with the prayer.

May I know I am lovable.

I closed my eyes as tears overtook me again. Was I lovable or was I just weird? Did all those taunting children back in grade school know something I didn't know? Perhaps I still needed to become someone I wasn't. Or was I actually okay just like this?

I moved on to the last line of the prayer and spoke it out loud. "May I love and be loved with ease."

Ease. I didn't know what this was when it came to love. I knew compatibility and deep friendship, like I had with my husband. But ease? True, lasting, deep, intimate love...with ease?

Was it even possible? Did I deserve this, too?

I prayed and prayed that day, repeating the Metta Prayer as my tears lifted and my voice took on a low, meditative sing-song.

May I be happy
May I know my true worth
May I know I am lovable
May I love and be loved with ease

At the end of ten minutes, I opened my eyes and looked out at the pond beyond my window. My heart felt genuinely lighter, and more at peace. And once again, I did, indeed, feel worthy.

The Metta was already working its beautiful magic.

I walked downstairs in my pajamas. As usual, Linda was at her post at the dining room table diligently working, though it wasn't yet seven-thirty. She glanced up from her keyboard and smiled.

"Hey Lin, do you think I'm lovable?" I asked. Linda regarded me with a look of mild outrage at the very injustice of the question.

"Suzanne! Of course you're lovable!" she burst. "I mean, you're like *seriously* lovable."

"Oh, okay," I said. "Just checking."

But of course, I needn't have asked. There was only one person who could truly answer that question.

And that was me.

CHAPTER TWELVE

A s my days unfolded with no work to do, I began to worry about money.

It had been nearly a year since I had stopped working and my funds were dwindling. I began to accept a few business coaching clients, though I knew in my heart I was scarcely able to help them. Our sessions did not go well. But by this point, I had to do *something*. Or so it seemed.

After all, money wasn't going to just show up magically...was it?

As if on cue, my Guides started lining up one by one, lecturing me about trusting my path. As in trusting the *right* path.

I had a vivid pair of dreams. In one, I was in a yoga class struggling to maintain a one-legged balance pose. All of a sudden, I relaxed and let go. I stopped trying so hard. And in that instant, I rose up into the air and began to fly around the room.

"This is it!" I cried giddily to no one. "This is it!"

I had a deep sense of rightness. It was as if I had been delivered exactly where I was meant to be.

In the second dream, I was standing at an intersection in the middle of Sebastopol. My spirit guides were there, and they were training me to grow bigger, to expand. Arrows painted in an intersection at the very center of the town showed me which way to go. The path to my expansion was clearly marked; I simply needed to follow it.

Yet, despite the clarity of my dreams, I still didn't get it. I couldn't see that the Universe had my back in this critical time of grief. I couldn't see that I was protected and taken care of. Instead, I was still following my old Pavlovian response. *Do something.* I continued to scramble for paying work by offering specials. Yet the two clients I secured both stopped working with me, demanding refunds within weeks.

A few days later, I found myself pouring my worries out to God. *I feel so hopeless right now—like I am going to die penniless, a bereft, broken failure,* I typed onto a blank document. *How am I going to send Luke to college? Or even survive for that matter?*

The reply from Spirit was swift and concise. And consoling.

Pushing the rock up the hill won't always get you to the top. You are better left alone sometimes, just to give yourself what you need.

You will prevail. You will find your audience. You will find your work. You will find your way to the next level of karmic evolution. You will find your right gifts to give in this lifetime.

It is all preordained and you have nothing to do but trust that you are worthy for this task.

For that is what you doubt most right now...that you are worthy.

Are you worthy, Suzanne?

Are you truly worthy of this work that has been given to you?

I stopped writing and sat back. This had been the message in the Metta Prayer as well.

Spirit continued. *Will you surrender completely? Because nothing less is required here.*

If you don't let go and trust fully, you cannot receive fully.

Once more the message had appeared. The way to heal, to actually find my self-worth, was by doing...nothing. It would happen simply by surrendering to the inevitable course of life, and letting it carry me in its swift-moving river.

It was still a concept I could barely understand.

Letting go meant not having a to-do list every day. It meant not thinking out every possible outcome in advance. Not trying to strategize or manipulate my way to success. I had to rewrite the fundamental instructions I'd lived my entire life with.

If there was a bigger work of some kind for me to do, I would only find it by following the instincts and needs that bubbled up in my body and my heart.

I thought of something Teal had written in one of the journals she left behind.

Fear is just another way of saying No. Practice Yes in all areas of your life to learn to let it go.

Practice Yes.

Perhaps it really was that simple.

"Been cleaning house all day," began the psychic with a laugh. "But come on then, let's begin." She picked up the tarot cards and shuffled as I smiled at the Skype screen. Joanne Gregory, the British psychic who had read my cards so powerfully the previous year, was back, this time at her own request.

"I am being guided to gift you a reading," was how she put it, and of course I eagerly accepted. Joanne began by talking about money and work. "You're trying many things right now," she observed. "But two projects will come to the forefront and provide your livelihood when the time is right."

It was good news that Joanne saw relief ahead.

One type of work was, as she put it, "something healing that has to do with Teal." The other work was more businesslike, involving a business plan. "Jack or Josh will offer you something in about four months," she said vaguely. Then she paused. "It's work you used to do in the past," she said. "This project is worth doing."

Now I was confused. None of this seemed to jive with my current plans—to gingerly re-launch a key part of the Internet Marketing business I'd abandoned when Teal died. Somehow, despite all the guidance I'd received to the contrary, I thought I could still dredge up the overblown sales pages of my former life.

Joanne continued. "Teal says don't get frustrated if you don't get results right away. Even if you're feeling weak and overworked."

She looked at the cards a moment longer. "That's nice," she murmured. "Teal is giving you a handful of embroidered hearts."

Immediately I flashed to a waking vision I'd had a few days prior. In it I saw a framed picture of myself, looking especially joyful. I watched as pink hearts embroidered themselves around the photograph.

"Really, the big message here is that there is a love partnership for you. This is substantial. A proper love," Joanne said, looking up. "Have you met someone already?"

I'd gone on a handful of dates under the watchful eye of my dating coaches Ruth and Max. Available women had started showing up right on schedule, but none had been a fit so far. At the moment, I was getting to know a woman who was a sergeant in the San Francisco Police Department. We'd been circling each other with interest, though it was unclear if we were meant to date or just be friends.

"I think this woman is in law or possibly transport," said Joanne.

Law?

"Wait, really?" I asked.

This news was surprising. Helen, the cop, definitely

intrigued me. She was a fascinating, impressive woman who'd flown helicopters and chased criminals on foot. But I wasn't sure we had enough chemistry or compatibility to actually make a relationship work. For starters, she got home from work every night at 3AM, and she tended to sleep with a loaded gun by her bed.

"I've been getting to know a police officer. Could it be her?" I asked.

"What's her name?" Joanne asked and I told her.

Joanne shook her head. "No, I'm getting a D name." She looked off into the distance. "Deborah," she said. "She's an older person…or perhaps younger. There's an age difference. As long as she can be herself, and you can be you, you and Deborah will be very happy together for the rest of your life."

Deborah.

The possibility struck me. I was going to find someone named Deborah and spend the rest of my life with her? The thought was surprising, and yet it had the ring of truth also.

Why not, I thought. Suddenly I felt more ready than ever to fall in love.

I stared at the screen of my laptop and willed my eyes to stay open. My inner German soldier and I had been at it for hours. It was 11 PM and I was rewriting the copy of my sales page, just like the old days. Even though every fiber of my being resisted launching this course or this career again. Even though I'd clearly been told, repeatedly, to let go and trust. And even though my recent psychic reading suggested my effort would fail.

A friend of Linda's, an expert in online sales pages, peered over my shoulder. "People want to buy things that make them money," she'd stressed, pointing to my copy. "Beef up that part. Cut all this extra stuff."

The 'extra stuff' that now lay on the floor in tatters was my new, heart-based approach to life. It was the part about the path I'd been traveling for the last eighteen months. Still, if losing meant I could make some much-needed money, I'd hold my nose and try it.

Forty-eight hours later, the results were in. I'd sold sixteen of the programs, and made enough to get me through the next six months. Linda's friend was right. I wondered why I'd resisted this so much. Flooded with relief, I collapsed in bed, exhausted.

I woke up eight hours later to complete and total chaos. While I slept my site had been hacked and dismantled, including the interactive learning area for my new clients. Three of them were already demanding a refund.

For the next week, I watched helplessly as my tech assistant battled the voracious hackers who took down my site five more times. At one point malware even got deposited into my assistant's computer that began to eat everything in her hard drive.

By the end, my launch was destroyed and my former career was now finally, mercifully over. Almost gratefully I gave back every penny I had been paid and dismantled the ill-fated website.

A few days later, reality hit. I lay on the chaise and looked out the window of my tiny rented office, feeling hopeless, still unable to trust the Universe's plan for me. I began to cry, feeling as small and utterly alone as I ever had. I had my car, my borrowed room in Linda's home, some money for retirement, and a son who was busy with his own life 3,000 miles away. And that was it.

What was I going to do?

I still didn't fully believe that I could trust the Universe to take care of me, that I could find my way simply by following my heart. I looked out the window on the gray Sebastopol afternoon in despair, and as I did, a voice whispered in my ear. It was Teal.

Clean out your inbox, she said.

"What?" I asked aloud. "Honey, is that you?" The telltale crackle of her sparkling energy filled the room. Once again I could feel the pure, scintillating joy of Teal's presence as her high-pitched laughter ripped through me.

Clean out your inbox, she repeated.

"My inbox?" I murmured. I glanced over at the wire basket beside me. It was stacked high with documents, receipts, and the paperwork of daily life. I hadn't cleaned my inbox out since the year before Teal died. Instead, each time I'd moved, I'd simply shoved it and its ever-expanding contents into a waiting box.

"This inbox?" I asked uncertainly. "The one right here?" Teal's laughter rippled through me again in confirmation.

I sighed, reached for the first sheet of paper on top, and began sorting.

Two hours later, I looked up from my reverie. Receipts, invoices, instructions, mementos, letters, and more were now stacked into neat piles on the carpet all around me. I'd nearly gotten to the bottom of the inbox, but it still wasn't clear why she'd asked me to do this. I'd uncovered nothing of importance beyond papers waiting to be filed.

Still, one last remaining document lay on the bottom of the wire basket, face down. I pulled it out and turned it over. And in that moment, I understood completely what this exercise had been about.

In my hands was a letter Teal had written to me on our last Christmas together. This letter had been part of her gift to me. At the time, I'd stuck it in my inbox and promptly forgotten it.

Yet here it was now. And it was more precious than ever.

I began to read the letter once again.

Dear Mom,

Thanks for everything. I was trying to figure out what to get you, but all I could come up that I felt was good to spend money on was (you'll see). So I chose to also write you a note.

When I did my healing with Ambujam she pulled up all this stuff about you and me. She said basically in past lives we had always clashed, and in this life we are not supposed to. We are supposed to be leaders in love and light, supporting each other.

So from now on, I support any light leadership you have to bring to the world. And I'm currently on my spiritual healing discovery quest, so will see what comes out of it…

Soooo let's be leaders of/and in light! Ya!
Thanks for supporting me and all the love you send my way. I love you!

Teal

I put down the letter as sobs overtook me.

Of course we were supposed to be leaders in love and light. This was the articulation of the very thing I'd experienced as Teal lay dying in the hospital. This was the amorphous 'it' that I'd been looking for.

Here was my purpose in life, lying at the bottom of all of the junk of my daily life, waiting patiently for me to discover it. Only now was I ready for this awareness.

I thought back to Teal's psychic healings with Amubjam at my apartment, and her posting *I surrender* on her Facebook page.

It really was that simple.

Gently, I put the letter back in my inbox and regarded it. It was a powerful reminder not to give up hope. That I was, indeed, on the right track.

I had nothing to fear. All I needed to do was sit back, relax and enjoy the ride.

CHAPTER THIRTEEN

I t had been nearly a month since I'd found Teal's letter, and I
lay in bed in the dawn half-light. The winter pond outside
was nearly gone, and a late spring sunrise was spreading behind
the trees on the horizon.

I closed my eyes to rest, and as I did a vision swam up. It was
of the bathroom door just next to my bedroom. It was closed,
and radiant white light poured out around its edges, as if something very brilliant was inside.

I knew in an instant it was Teal.

"Are you there?" I asked.

I clearly heard her voice reply, *Yes.*

"Why won't you let me see you?" I asked.

I don't want you to get distracted.

I was quiet for an instant, absorbing the reality of the vision.
I could feel her nearness, her crackling energy all around me.
There was an aliveness in the air, as if every molecule was excited
by her presence.

"Do you have a message for me?" I asked.

The light around the bathroom door intensified slightly.

You are whole and complete and ready to go back to work. You have everything you need, and you need nothing more. You can begin now.

The vision disappeared.

I opened my eyes again and considered what had just happened. Of all the messages Teal could have given me at this moment, this was not one I would have expected.

But then, when I thought about it, I *was* whole and complete. I *was* ready to go back to work, not the stuff of my past but my true work. My body knew it, and I knew it. There was a completion and a new confidence now. Or maybe it was just a willingness that hadn't been there before.

I still wasn't clear on what that work was quite yet, but the fact that I was ready to do it was good news.

I climbed out of bed, excited, and hurried down the stairs to tell Linda.

Two weeks later an answer arrived as I sat at lunch with my cousin Jack.

He was eating blueberries, his usual lunch. Jack tasted a few with a lovely silver spoon, courtesy of the elegant men's club he belonged to. Around us portraits of patrician white men hung on the walls. On the table before me, creamy linens and fine china bore my lunch.

I took a bite of my Dover Sole.

"The thing is, after all of these years, I want to have some fun," he said, explaining his current situation. After decades of successful, dedicated work in finance, Jack had accumulated real wealth. And now he was ready for some genuinely fun creative projects.

"Specifically, I was thinking books," he said. "Novels."

"I'm listening," I replied.

"I've never forgotten your first book," he said, referring to a coming-of-age novel I published in 1990 that was now out of print. Out of a whoosh of timing, sheer luck, and a little talent, I'd managed to publish my first novel with a major publisher. The results of which were underwhelming.

"You mean the book nobody read?" I said with a smile.

"I read it," he persisted, "and I thought it very good. Suzanne, it occurred to me you'd be the perfect person to write this character I have in mind," he began.

Jack went on to explain an idea he'd had for a series of novels about a transman spy who embodied both masculine strength and feminine spirit and empathy. This spy lived squarely between genders and used both his physical power and his natural intuitive grace to be extremely good at his job.

I was intrigued.

"How many novels are we talking about?" I asked.

"Oh, I don't know. Six, maybe?" he told me. "I'm thinking of a series."

Now, nearly two years after Teal's death, I seriously needed to get back to work. Yet, my future as the purported 'leader in love and light' with Teal wasn't quite here yet, either. Could it be this was the interim assignment Joanne had described to me in her reading?

I looked out the window at Park Avenue below us and the sunlight painting the high rises all around us. "I'd need to have creative control," I said.

"You'd have it," he concurred.

"And the novels would have to be funny."

"Exactly," Jack agreed. "That's what I was thinking."

I looked at him. "And the terms?"

"We'll work something out," he said. "You would be paid for your work."

It sounded perfect, but somehow I still couldn't say yes. My heart was still too raw and my inertia still seemed weirdly necessary, as if it were protecting me somehow.

I knew I needed to go back to work, but writing fiction? Did I still have that particular spark within me?

"Let me think about it," I said.

Jack smiled, apparently satisfied. "Take your time," he said graciously. Then he returned to his blueberries.

The world, yet again, was working in mysterious ways.

———————

The Korean baths were nearly empty on a Saturday night, and I enjoyed the luxury of sitting alone in the steaming whirlpool. I'd come to San Francisco to attend a party in the neighborhood. But first, I stopped by the baths for some intensive self-care.

On the other side of the large, tiled room, an Asian woman who worked there quietly went about her business, picking up towels. The silence in the spa was deep and complete. I closed my eyes and sank a little more deeply into the hot, swirling water. I felt my whole body give way and relax, and as I did, I could feel Teal make her entrance.

Hello, love.

Hi, Mom.

Whatcha doing? I asked.

A small laugh bubbled through me. It was the usual Teal laughter for no reason other than the joy of being. On the other side of the room, the attendant looked up. She gave me a smile and I beamed back at her.

I'm preparing you, Teal continued.

Preparing me for what? I asked.

You'll see.

This time, instead of disappearing, she lingered for a while. Her presence soothed me as she suffused the whirlpool with her energy.

Sinking back into the pool, I surrendered all of my tension, my worries, and my sadness. Allowing it to swirl out of my body into the water, I let go. I breathed in the fizz of Teal's essence, the possibility, the joy and the pure love that she was now, my disembodied sparkle of a daughter.

Thank you, I murmured sometime later. She just glowed as a laugh pushed through me once more. Then she was gone.

Twenty minutes later, I walked up Filmore street to The Girl

Party. This massive, roaming party of lesbians happened every few months in some generous Bay Area person's private home. This time it was in San Francisco. I walked up to the doorway of the old Victorian and saw a friend just inside.

"Thank God you made it," she said. "This place is packed! The doors are just about to close."

I pushed into the house as lesbians of every description chatted, drank, and partied all around me. Tatted, pierced girls in their twenties danced while middle-aged women gossiped and older women sat together in the back on lawn chairs, watching and sipping wine.

I put my potluck offering down on a table in the backyard and looked around. One empty seat beckoned to me, a bench across from a few chatting women. One of the women looked up at me as I neared.

She was a beautiful and silver-haired, and her face glowed with the zest of a life well lived. "Join us," she said. We smiled at each other as I sat down across from her.

"We were just talking about a recent overnight we made to the hostel at Point Reyes. Are you a hiker?" she asked.

"I am," I replied.

We began to talk. Within a few more moments this mysterious silver-haired woman was sitting next to me, and our conversation had deepened. She began telling me about her adventures cycling twice across the country, solo hiking sections of the Pacific Crest Trail, and backpacking deep into the wilderness of the Sierras.

"Why backpack?" I asked. "Why not just car camp?"

She cocked her head and looked at me. "Have you ever backpacked?" she asked.

I replied that I never had.

"When you backpack, you can finally find the silence," she explained, her voice filled with rapture. "Imagine being in a place in nature where you are totally alone for days on end, where you can see every last star in the sky and there's no one else around for miles. I know places off the trail where nobody goes. Nobody at all," she assured me. I didn't doubt it.

I looked at her and something shifted inside of me. Who was this woman? I studied her, trying to understand what was happening as I became more and more enraptured with each purring, lilting word she spoke.

"Why are you telling me this?" I finally asked.

She looked at me levelly. "I'm looking for some activities we might do together," she explained calmly. Something in my groin stirred.

This is it, I thought to myself.

"What's your name?" I asked.

"Deborah," she replied.

Deborah! My mind sputtered and reeled, and I felt like I was waking up from a very long nap.

"I'm Suzanne," I said. A moment of silence ticked by as we looked at each other, recognizing something. I thought back to my last reading with Joanne.

There was once last acid test. My true love was supposed to be in law—or possibly transportation.

"And what do you do for a living, Deborah?" I asked.

She smiled and looked down. "Oh, I'm a lawyer, but I'm retiring," she said. Then she glanced up brightly. "In my heart of hearts, I want to be a conductor on Amtrak," she added with a laugh.

A shot of electricity poured through my body in confirmation. Yes, this really was it.

My love had arrived.

I glanced around me, struck by the extraordinary normality of all of this. Of course, this woman, this Deborah I'd been hearing about, was now sitting right beside me. And of course we had found each other. We would now begin our path together, one foot in front of the other, heading straight for the unfiltered sunlight.

The Universe really *did* have my back.

I smiled back at Deborah. "So glad to hear it," I managed to say.

My future had just officially begun.

CHAPTER FOURTEEN

I opened my email and ran a cursory scan through the inbox. An unfamiliar set of words caught my eye.

Correspondence from Teal's Heart/Kidney Recipient, it said.

I stopped and stared at my email as an overwhelming urge to cry rushed through my body. Here was the letter we had been hoping for during the last year; some kind of accounting, on paper, that in the end Teal's death had not been in vain.

Quickly I clicked on the email and began to read. Almost simultaneously, I began to sob.

We knew that Teal's heart and kidney had gone to a young woman close to her age, though we knew little else about her. I'd imagined her to be a young woman with ongoing medical problems just like Teal, so a new heart could truly save her life. Someone who, like Teal, had lingered on the brink of death.

I imagined that she, too, had a mother who sat by her bedside, holding her hand and trying to understand how God could let this happen to someone so young. But unlike Teal, she had not let go and traveled to the afterlife. Instead, this young woman had been given a second chance.

Now here she was, writing to say thank you.

Nearly a year earlier, Larry had insisted on writing a tender, eloquent letter to Teal's three organ recipients. He shared who Teal was in detail: all of her quirks, her passions, her love for travel, and her overflowing heart. And he encouraged them to write back or even to meet us if they were so moved. If they did, he promised, we would welcome them with open arms.

No one had come forth until now.

Slowly, I read the recipient's letter, tears streaming down my face.

I cannot express how happy I am to hear from you, it began. *I have been trying to put my letter together for so long, not even knowing where to begin, and in that time coming to the conclusion that there is only one place to start: Thank You.*

Thank you so much for you and your family's selfless decision, which I am positive was one of the hardest decisions you have ever made, to let your daughter live on through other people.

I paused and took a breath. My heart was beating right out of my chest. No, I wanted to shout. No, it wasn't hard at all! It was easy to donate Teal's organs and tissues, and it was absolutely what was meant to be.

The decision to donate had been completely guided on that fateful day. It was just one more piece of my daughter's destiny, and so it became ours as well.

My name is Amera, the letter continued, *and I am the recipient of your daughter's heart and kidney. I was nineteen years old when I was diagnosed with congestive heart failure. I have endured several surgeries and many bad days, but I have continued to stay positive throughout this adventure that is my life.*

I am now 28, happy, healthy, going to school, hiking with my animals, and doing my best to live my life to the fullest. I have vowed not to take anything for granted. Of course, I have my days, as I am only human. However, my bad days are a small bump in the road compared to what they once were.

God bless her, I thought. What a horrible thing to live with when you are only nineteen years old. It had to be like Teal's epilepsy, shaping the basic decisions she made every single day.

Having a transplant has changed my life in every way. I now have the energy and stamina to do the things that for so long I was unable to do. I love the outdoors, I love my animals. I plan to buy a piece of property when I am done school, and have a lot more animals.

Traveling is also a love of mine. I love anywhere tropical and plan to travel as much as possible in the future. I found it very inspiring that Teal also loved to travel. That makes my desire to see the world even stronger. I would be very honored if my next big adventure could be to meet you and your family.

I am so honored you have reached out to me and my family. It has moved us in ways that words cannot describe.

Of course, I thought with a smile. Teal's heart recipient was given the gift of travel as a result of Teal's death. I thought of all of those trips throughout the world Teal took with just her backpack and her small busking guitar. It was never enough for her to stay parked in Essex or San Francisco. She had to see the world. And now this small piece of her would, indeed, carry on.

Amera went on to describe how she was studying to become a diagnostic imaging technician, hopefully at the hospital where she received her transplant. *It would mean so much to be able to give back to the establishment and the wonderful staff who saved my life*, she wrote.

I smiled to myself. Teal wanted to be a healer, and here we were again.

Amera closed by saying this:

I have spoken to many of my fellow transplant recipients who have never had contact with their donor families. It thrills me to have this opportunity and I will cherish it always and hope to keep in touch in the future. It may sound strange, but I feel like your daughter and I would have been good friends if given the chance. She is part of me, and I will be forever grateful.

She closed by wishing us all peace and happiness. Then she added one last beautiful line:

...I will never take for granted what she has given me.

I leaned back on the chaise lounge and began to cry, not from grief over Teal's death but rather because of the great magnitude of life. This big sweeping arc of love that encompasses us all is always there. I could feel this more deeply than ever.

We are all one, every last one of us. I knew that now in a way I never had before.

It had to be true, for we all share the same beating hearts. And if one person's organs can slip seamlessly into another person's body and give them life, then we truly are one. No matter where we come from or what we believe.

There is no difference between any of us, as the gift of Teal's big, beautiful heart confirmed. Any differences we imagine are merely cosmetic.

So now Amera was in my life, whether we ever met in person or not. Teal's legacy was complete. It was a gift that transcended all time.

Just like Amera, I, too, would never take anything for granted again.

Change your will to a chorus of love, a voice boomed in my dream. It boomed loudly enough to wake me up. It was all I could remember.

Change your will to a chorus of love. What exactly did that mean?

Instant knowing flooded my body and lit up my senses. My will—that good old German Soldier—was still in there, though remarkably less stern and forbidding lately. I suspected she might even be starting to relax.

Changing my will now meant changing the anxious, forceful part of me that was filled with fear and a damning shame when I didn't strive, accomplish, and achieve. Perhaps my soldier had to have one last stand before her complete and total annihilation.

And what in God's name was a 'chorus of love?' Immediately an angelic choir popped into my head, full of tow-headed cherubs, all rosy-cheeked and bedecked in pink ribbons. In an instant I got it. This was a perfect chorus of *self-love.*

I wondered if such a change was possible. It certainly seemed like the next step.

I began the chorus in my head.

I am enough.
I am doing enough.
I will always be enough, just as I always have been.

I was starting to get the message. I really was worthy of love and trust. I was no longer a pretend leader hoping no one would look behind the curtains. Nor was I a bully leader judging those who didn't love every word that issued from my mouth.

I was no longer the egoic leader who was just in it for the spotlight and the praise. And I was no longer the shallow leader wanting to grab as much cash as I could.

Now, instead, I stood naked before the world. I was vulnerable and afraid, but still willing. This was the process of learning to just be.

This was what Teal had been talking about all along.

The message of the dream was now clear. Heal yourself, and as you do, make love to the world just as your heart has always wanted.

I had a direct experience of this new compassion in Oakland the following week. It was a Sunday morning, and I'd just run around Lake Merritt. I was making my way back to Deborah's house, blissed out on pheromones, when I passed a homeless man sitting on a milk crate. He was selling copies of *Street News*. A hand-lettered sign in front of him read: *Please give what you can. (12 Years Sober.)*

Immediately I stopped. Here was a brother. I smiled, as did he. I noticed the skin on his old Black hands was calloused and worn. He'd clearly been on the streets for years. A tall plastic cup of something red and slushy sat beside him on the sidewalk.

"Congratulations on your sobriety. That's great," I said. Then I sat down beside him.

He beamed and began digging in his pockets with shaky hands. "Let me show you," he said proudly. It took a minute or two for him to extract an old, worn wallet from his pocket. The contents issued forth all over the sidewalk. I helped him pick it up: an ID, a Medicare card, the assorted pieces of paper required to move a person through a system.

"Here they are!" he said triumphantly. He held out two bronze disks. I took them and carefully examined them. They were his eleven- and twelve-year AA chips for maintaining his sobriety.

We chatted about recovery groups for a few moments. "The kindest people in the world," I said. He agreed.

I bought a few copies of his newspaper. "What's your name?" he asked and I told him. We smiled at each other, now friends. I was quite sure I'd bump into him again. I held out my hand. "I'm so glad to meet you," I said. His hand fit into mine and we shook.

"See you around."

"Yep. See you around. Take care."

"You take care."

It was an encounter I would never have had before Teal's death. I would have been too busy, too self-involved, too locked into a lock-step life of striving, pushing for that million-dollar schema in the sky. That was really all that mattered then.

But now I understood. Everything I could reasonably hope for in this life was right here, in this tender moment. I'd become someone who was free enough to walk down the street and find love staring out at me, waiting for me to discover it.

It was like I finally, truly had enough. Though on paper I barely had anything at all.

If I could keep the chorus of love going who knew where it would lead?

A few days later Deborah and I walked on a beach at dusk. Waves moved in, splashing our naked legs, the water becoming warmer as we walked on and on. Sea stacks, rock formations that were thousands of years old, rose around us like obscure obelisks. The beach was deserted.

"I've decided I just want to help one person at a time," she said. "That's all I can do. And isn't that enough?" she asked.

A wave moved in around our legs, sweeping us clean. We held on to each other a little tighter. "Yeah," I agreed. "It's enough." The gentle truth was seeping in: we didn't have to be any more than we were in this moment.

I could feel my soul relax. There is no 'there' to get to anymore. All that striving and pushing, all that anxiously trying to hide my true being was simply an illusion.

We are born of light and back to light we would return. This much Teal had taught me in her life and in her death. So I vowed to keep on dissolving, finding my way back to that light, one beautiful step at a time.

The chorus of love could now sing on forever, in a world that truly was without end.

CHAPTER FIFTEEN

The Northern California day was sunny, crisp and perfectly temperate, and a bright wind swirled in from the Pacific. Today Deborah and I were riding our bikes out to the Pacific Coast Highway.

Cycling was something I kept meaning to do since I moved to California, but grief and procrastination had benched me. Yet now I'd taken up with a serious cyclist, so riding was an obvious date choice. At age sixty-three, Deborah was still doing century rides of sixty-five miles. Meanwhile, I was good for ten, maybe twenty miles. If that.

We rode along a winding road out to the sea, surrounded by wildflowers. An occasional car passed, but the way was easy and the pace relaxed. This was the kind of cycling I liked. As we descended a long hill, Deborah hunkered down into a tuck, sped up, and disappeared. Meanwhile, I braked my way cautiously down the hill, nervous as ever about going too fast.

Still, I was here, I told myself. That was the important thing. It was okay if I couldn't keep up. I was doing just fine. And besides, Deborah really was incredibly hot in her bike shorts.

Eventually, I caught sight of her ahead, waiting patiently by the side of the road. "Are you okay with me riding ahead?" she asked, as I pulled up to a stop.

"Yep," I replied, wiping the sweat from my face. "You know I can't begin to keep up with you."

"That's fine," she said with a smile. "I was just showing off."

We laughed. "Yeah, well, you look pretty damn good," I told her.

"So do you," she replied, and I smiled shyly. Pretty much everything this woman said undid me.

Together we picked up speed and flew past the small houses, and then the bigger and bigger eucalyptus trees. Then we turned onto Highway One and headed north toward Jenner, and that's when everything changed.

Immediately an eighteen-wheeler roared past us, filling my face with road dust. I blinked and pressed on, determined to keep up. We began to pump up a long, painful hill as a steady roar of traffic kept up on our left.

I began to feel shakier and shakier. Meanwhile, Deborah pulled ahead and disappeared while I began to ride more and more slowly. Finally I got out and walked my bike up the last of the hill. My butt seriously hurt, and I hoped we could turn around soon. I imagined we were at least twenty miles into our ride.

Deborah stopped up ahead and waited for me. "How far have we ridden?" I asked, panting as I reached her.

"Seven point five miles," she said. Then she looked at me with concern. "How are you doing?"

I was silent for a moment. Was I going to cave and admit to my lack of conditioning, my sore butt, and my abject terror of Highway One? Was I going to actually take care of myself first?

Was that really okay to be honest with this woman whom I was slowly, gingerly learning to trust?

"This is the first time I've ridden my bike in a really long time. It's been at least a couple of years," I panted. "Anyway, I'm afraid out here," I finally admitted.

"I was wondering about that," Deborah said. "Well, no worries. We'll turn around."

It was agreed that I would ride back downhill to the nearest town, and she would go retrieve the car where we started. Then she would come get me.

I pumped away on my bike feeling slightly mortified. How could I have pulled the plug on our lovely ride? But at the same time, part of me was vastly relieved. I was grateful that I'd had the courage to speak up.

The world had not ground to a halt. The sky didn't fall. Instead, a kind person listened without judgment and met my request. She didn't even seem remotely bothered by it. Perhaps the world was far safer than I thought.

Half an hour later, we were back in the car. As we pulled away, Deborah glanced over at me. "Thank God you said something," she remarked. "Not everyone would, you know. They'd be too busy being tough."

"Apparently that part of me is gone," I remarked.

"That took courage," she said. Then she reached over and squeezed my hand.

I smiled as we drove back toward Sebastopol. Life was meeting me now, as I showed up more and more fully every day. Once again I'd discovered that it really was okay to be me.

Not only was it okay, it was actually required. And so the Universe could provide what I'd been asking for.

A real and lasting love.

Highway 101 South unfolded before me as I drove to a meeting with my fellow debtors. I watched the gradual easing of countryside flow into suburbia. I relaxed as I drove. And I thought about my finances.

I considered the obvious: going back to work writing novels with my cousin. It had been on my mind a lot since his offer the previous month. I'd been living on financial vapors for far too long, refusing every extra expense and counting every last penny. I seriously needed to earn some money again.

But still, I hesitated.

What held me back now was a fear that I couldn't deliver. I had been in my healing cocoon for nearly two years. What if I wrote a mediocre novel, or worse, what if no one bought these books? What if I got bad reviews?

The open highway moving beneath my wheels, the music pouring through the stereo, and California's brown hills rising around me began to work their magic. Soon, in came Radio Teal. The experience was both electrifying and grounding at the same time.

Teal was nothing but 1,000-watt happiness. She swirled through my consciousness like liquid nitrogen, or molten dark chocolate, or pure, melted sunshine.

"Honey?" I said aloud. "Are you there?"

A crystalline laugh slipped from my mouth. Though, as usual, nothing was particularly funny.

"So, what do you think?" I asked. "Should I work for Jack writing these novels?"

Teal's laughter rippled through me in angelic confirmation. *As if you didn't know,* I heard her say.

Yeah, of course. Okay. I knew I should do this work. I'd known it back in Jack's club when he proposed the idea in the first place. Yet the inertia of grief still held me fast that afternoon.

I was scared.

It had been a long time since I'd stopped working. I could go on like this indefinitely, living on savings, hiding out and barely existing. Or I could rise up, say yes to this offer, and begin to function once again as a working member of society.

Which was it going to be?

I thought of a recent dream in which I was shown a small, very strong metal safety bar. It was floating in mid-air beside me and I could grab onto it when I needed. I knew it would always be there, supporting me along the way.

"All right," I said aloud to no one. "I'll do it."

A small, silvery Teal laugh erupted and then drifted away.

I recalled the words of Joanne, the British psychic. She predicted that I would work with someone named Jack or Josh in four months' time. "It will be different from the work with Teal," she had said, "but it will be work worth doing." Now here we were four months later, right on schedule.

I resolved to call Jack that afternoon and say yes.

Whole Foods seemed an unlikely place to have a denouement. Yet, here I was, sipping my cold brew in the homey little café, and doing my best to evolve.

Once again, I was working on a critical step in my financial recovery work, examining my character defects, seeing what they cost me, and taking responsibility for them, one by one. I'd done this work before, but things still felt incomplete. So I was doing it again.

The questions my recovery work gave me to journal about pulled no punches.

Where in your life have you made material things most important? Where have you used people to get ahead? Where have you been controlling or needy?

And the worst one of all: *How has this affected your life and your relationships?*

It was slow work answering these questions. But it was also critical work because this was the stuff I avoided thinking about. Yet, it was also the sludge that weighed me down, the toxic gray matter that silently suffocated. To know it was to heal it.

I worked along, sipping my coffee and taking my time. One by one, I cataloged the moments in my life that filled me with shame. Calling up banks in a panic or ranting at tellers like a loose cannon. Wildly overcharging for my coaching work in search of money and validation. And pushing, needling, and cajoling everyone around me to serve my agenda and mine alone.

It was the German Soldier catalog. As usual.

I thought about my son when he was six years old, bounding up to my office after he got home from school, a little blond guy bursting with love and eager to play. Instead of taking a twenty-minute break to have some fun, I would tell him firmly, "Mommy has to work now. You can be in my office but only if you do your homework."

The fact was Mommy was just a little too self-important back then to show her son the kindness and love he deserved on those weekday afternoons. I could have taken a half-hour break to spend time with him, but I didn't. It was a habit that now filled me with shame.

And I remembered a conversation with Teal, when she asked me for a pair of new shoes for her work as a barista. "I'm on my feet all the time, Mom. These aren't going to cut it," she said, pointing to the worn-out Keds she always wore. At this point, her cheap canvas sneakers were barely holding together.

Instead of embracing the chance to be supportive and give my daughter some new shoes, I hesitated. I told her I wasn't sure I could afford it.

"Mom," she said, looking me square in the face. "You make plenty of money and you certainly can afford it."

I knew she was right, of course. Just as I knew 'I can't afford it' was a weirdly frequent refrain in my life. Even when I was earning hundreds of thousands of dollars every year. Even when the rational part of my brain knew it wasn't true.

Then there was my wild overspending on my business. Going through the books made me shake my head. $18,000 for an audio crew in the back of a workshop for 100 people. $5,000 for a wardrobe consultant to make me look 'professional.' What in God's name had I been thinking? *It's only money,* I told myself at the time.

In fact, it was grandiosity and total overkill. And it was insane.

Before recovery, a fog of oblivion descended on me when I thought about my money. Rather than check my bank balances, I'd guess at them, honestly believing I had a second sense that knew exactly how much I had in the bank at any given time. Such vagueness meant I could spend money however and whenever I wished, without apparent consequences. Except for the part that there always were consequences—bad ones. This habit kept me mired in five-figure debt throughout my adult life.

At the same time, I'd overworked compulsively as well, with a relentless, driven pace that burned through reasonable time. When I was working, I demanded miracles from myself, instantly or at the very latest overnight. I expected the same from my assistants, which explained why I'd cycled through eight of them in six years.

The list of my transgressions was long and gnarly. Still, it felt good to finally face them and write them all down. For now I could begin to understand what drove these habits. And I could take responsibility where I'd caused harm, make my amends, and so forgive myself. Just as God already had.

I stirred my coffee as I sat there in the café, mulling over my list.

In the end, all of it had been motivated by need. The need to be special, to be perfect. To be seen by the world. My appetite for recognition was voracious, and I stopped at nothing to get it…even ignoring my children's needs.

Finally I could see how relentlessly driven I had been.

I looked out the window of Whole Foods to Bay Street, taking a breather from the insights that now fell like dominos in front of me. My eyes fell on the billboard affixed to the building directly across the street. It nearly took my breath away.

You don't need to be famous to be unforgettable, the billboard read.

In the picture, an adult and a child were bent in concentration together over a project.

No, Suzanne, you don't need to be famous. Nor do you need to be perfect, be a star or be anything other than what you are right now. The fact is, you can just breathe and relax into the gift of this life.

Then you can approach the rest of the world with all the love that's in your heart. You can find your way back to right service, helping people however you are meant to. And you don't have to worry for one minute about whether you are known, or not known, or have done the job perfectly.

Yet again, Teal's message came back to me. You are enough, just as you are, Suzanne.

Just be.

CHAPTER SIXTEEN

I punched the number into my cell phone and waited, barely breathing. My heart was pounding hard, and part of me hoped there would be no answer. I was calling Amera, Teal's heart recipient.

It had been a year since we had gotten her letter, and I'd emailed her twice to no reply. Yet that afternoon I suddenly realized I'd been sending my emails to the wrong email address. But then, that was grief for you. Always throwing the wool over your eyes.

I called Amera as soon as she emailed back with her number.

The phone rang. Then it rang again. A young woman's voice came on the line.

"Amera?" I asked.

"Yes?"

"It's Suzanne, Teal's mom."

Immediately, I began to cry. I found I could not speak. For a long moment neither of us could. It sounded like she was crying, too.

"I'm sorry I screwed up on sending the email," I blubbered. "And I'm sorry I'm crying!" I said with a laugh.

"It's okay," Amera said shakily. "I am too."

My words burst out of me. "This is like…kryptonite."

The emotional intensity of speaking to Teal's heart recipient now slammed me right between the eyes. Intellectually, it had all seemed like a perfect, appropriate thing to do. A right thing to do.

But in this moment, I was talking to living, breathing Amera, the woman whose life had been saved by Teal's death and by our decision. Her very aliveness confronted me on the phone, and my entire central nervous system was on fire—a four-alarm fire.

Words were difficult, and for a long moment neither of us said much. Then finally, we began to talk. Once I got over the very fact of Amera and our connection, I started to relax.

I was reminded of the reaction of my grief group when I first heard from her a year earlier. Back then I was meeting weekly with other parents who'd lost children in a group sponsored by the local hospice. When I shared that I had unexpectedly gotten a letter from Teal's heart and kidney recipient, the response in the room was universal.

"She's still alive!" they all said. For this was the most fervent hope of every single person in that room. Despite the sheer impossibility of it, all we wanted was to have our children back.

So here was Amera. And somehow, just as a healer had predicted just after her death, here was Teal as well.

Even if only a few parts of her body still circulated blood and did their job every day, the physical reality of Teal hadn't completely slipped away. Somewhere her precious DNA still walked this earth.

So Amera and I talked for a while, and I remembered so poignantly of the sweetness of talking to young women. I missed these conversations terribly. But now I had reconnected to this younger world again, and I was grateful.

We hung up that day promising to meet each other the following month. Yet, the very intensity of our connection and this unlikely link between two perfect but destined strangers, made me suspect it might not happen.

Here we both were, lingering at the edge of life and earth, a place most people chose not to visit.

Yet this was exactly where life's greatest riches lived and breathed.

The sun poured down and glittered on the water of the Ives Pool as I stroked my way through my laps. The warm, lovely salt water comforted me as I swam. *I will miss it,* I thought, when I moved to Oakland.

Wait, who said I was moving to Oakland?

My thought surprised me, but it also made me smile. Since the second week of our relationship, I hadn't doubted that Deborah and I would live together. In fact, it seemed inevitable that we would marry. It even seemed that we'd been married before, in other lifetimes. This was just another indelible fact of life, like the predictable shrieks of the kids coming from the children's pool.

An image came to me from the previous weekend: dancing in a sea of bobbing, jubilant lesbians in Deborah's living room. Deborah had parties, big ones. And she had a lot of friends, including the half-dozen musicians who held forth that night, wailing on the sax, the bass, the piano, the drums, all collectively tearing up the place.

That night I felt myself swept up in the embrace of something bigger than just me. For thirty plus years, Deborah had been steadily building community. She knew everybody and everybody knew her. Now, set down in the midst of all of this, I felt like a part of something bigger again. I felt seen and heard and understood. But most of all, my face hurt from smiling.

Not one iota of this new, emerging life seemed anything less than perfect. I thought of our hikes, our bike rides, and of backpacking together in the Emigrant Wilderness. And our walks with the German Shepherd Athena as the evening set in over the Oakland hills.

I thought of sunny Saturday mornings, lying in her bed, softly enfolded together. And of my drives back and forth between Oakland and Sebastopol, when I sped along 101, once again alive like I hadn't been in years.

I thought of Teal's fizzy glow joining me in those love-lit rides home. One morning I snapped on the car stereo to hear Teal, herself, singing "Hallelujah." The rightness of it made me cry.

I was so lit from within by this woman. When I walked into a room and saw Deborah standing there, my heart turned over in my chest. As the months wore on, these feelings just became more intense, more real, and more suffused with love.

Nothing about Deborah was conventional, but then neither was I. Somehow we met on this other plane of 'us-ness,' our own little zone of the things we both loved: words, music, books, politics, and a thousand indescribable experiences that had somehow woven us together. And we talked and talked and talked some more, knowing we would never run out of great conversation.

When I took her hand and looked at the fading tattoo of flowers that had marked her wrist for decades, somehow, I knew her deeply. Deborah was mine and I was hers. The inevitable had been borne out once again. We had found each other in the random stream of life, and now we weren't letting go, no matter what.

All the yoga, prayer, meditation, and meetings; the grieving, journaling, dreaming and telling the truth about my life. Even the falling apart and the coming back together again. All of it had led me to this next happy conclusion.

I had come back to myself, and I could begin a brand-new life.

I reached the end of the pool, then hoisted myself out and

sat on the edge. As I did, I was flooded with gratitude. For Linda, who'd invited me to live with her, and for Divina, Ming Yang, my therapist, my sister Sarah, Andrea, the organ procurement agency, Jon, my recovery pals, Kashi. Even Anya.

I felt love for all of my friends in California, Paris, and in my programs, who'd guided me through my healing, my grief, my rebirth.

None of this would ever have happened if I'd remained alone and isolated in my pain. I needed every last one of these people to help me through.

In some ways, this was the greatest gift of all, to be able to ask for support and get it. And to feel their true and abiding love. To dance in the center of this new pack of friends, knowing that I truly belonged. I no longer needed to pretend to be someone other than who I was. Instead, I could give myself the gift of Grace. And I could look into my lover's eyes and know I was truly seen.

This was my reality now. In surrendering, I had, indeed, found my way home.

The outreach coordinator's voice was warm and cordial on the phone. I'd just told her about speaking to Amera and how much it meant to me.

"I am so very happy for you," she remarked. "I really hope you get to meet each other."

I stood in a patch of sunlight on the oriental rug in my office, studying its play against the carpet's bright colors. "I really have to thank you, Karen. You've helped our family so much."

This woman, in her even-handed kindness, still called both Larry and I from time to time, checking in to see how we were doing. She had found us hospice therapists, grief groups, sent helpful fliers, and genuinely cared about us in the two years since Teal's death. We were both truly grateful to her.

"I want to volunteer for your organization," I heard myself say. "I just want to give back. Is there some way for me to do that?"

I was a little surprised at myself. Where had this come from? Until that moment, I'd never given any thought to volunteering with the organ procurement agency.

"Absolutely," said Karen enthusiastically. "We have a lot of ways you can help, but you're a speaker, aren't you?"

"Yes, I am," I replied. *How did she know that?*

Karen was momentarily taken aback. "I don't know why I just asked you that," she said with a laugh. "Are you really a speaker?"

"I am. I've had a career speaking and leading workshops."

She chuckled. "Well, that's pretty perfect, because we never get to hear from Donor Moms. Are you giving any talks any time soon that I could attend?"

In fact, I was. One week earlier, Kashi had asked me to lead a workshop in her yoga studio. It was to be about self-care and finding joy after grief. It was the first speaking gig I'd taken since Teal's death.

The timing of all of this was remarkable. I gave Karen the time and date, and she said she'd be there.

I hung up and marveled at the synchronicity.

———

I sat in my car outside the café as a steady rain beat on the windshield. And as I did, tears slid down my face.

I was listening to an interview with an author talking about the criminalization of Black girls in high schools in America. Girls who were truant because they are being trafficked for sex. Girls who were being bullied and raped. Girls who got arrested where other girls might just be expelled.

I wanted to get out of the damp, chilly car and go into the café. After all, I needed to order my coffee and get back to work...didn't I? But now, somehow, in this new, more tender iteration of my life, I couldn't turn off the radio.

Instead, I found myself dialing into the show to speak with the author. An operator answered and put me on hold. A moment later, the host came on the line.

"Hello and who is this?"

"Suzanne from Oakland," I said.

"Go ahead, Suzanne."

I hesitated. I didn't even have a question, but there was so much to say. Somehow I knew these girls like I knew my own daughter, even though their life experiences had been completely different. In that moment, I could feel their pain and the rightness of reaching out.

"I have been so moved by what you are talking about..." I fumbled, and again tears welled up. "I'd like to help, but is there actually a way?" I finally croaked.

The speaker thanked me and told me to connect with my local school board and bring her book to their attention. Which seemed like the least I could do. And yet I had to wonder. Would my small actions seriously make any difference?

I could feel automatic hopelessness pour through me. *Nothing I could do would really matter.* But then I thought of Teal and her love for Black culture. Even though she was White and grew up in a place where African-Americans were few and far between. When she was five, she announced to a babysitter, "I'm going to be a singer when I grow up. A *Black* singer!"

It was this love that drove her to spend several months in Ghana when she was seventeen. There she saw the burning of the rain forest and poverty she couldn't even fathom. She also saw the buildings where more than six million slaves were housed before being shipped to America. And she found her way to a classroom to teach English to Ghanaian kids. But instead, they taught her to speak their language, Twee.

This love was what made Teal sing the blues, day after day on her small guitar. After her death, we heard from her vocal performance teacher at Berklee. She wrote to us, *Teal connected with blues through her compassion for other people's struggles… they gave her blues interpretations such passionate authenticity.*

Teal got the Black struggle in ways that I never had. In my White privilege, I had seldom given such matters much thought at all. Yet Teal had not only given it all a great deal of thought, she'd been moved to action.

Now I got out of the car and walked into the café, still fairly sure any calls I made to local school boards would yield nothing. I ordered my coffee, then I stopped. One of Teal's favorite songs was playing on the café sound system.

A moment later I sat down, turned on my computer, and typed in the name of the interviewer's book. The sales page immediately popped up and I began to read about it.

Then just as suddenly, out of nowhere, a new browser window opened. I watched, dumbfounded, as it magically loaded a new web page. It was the website for Tartine, the bakery and café where we celebrated Teal's last birthday together. It was one of her favorite places in San Francisco.

I hadn't typed in the web address, nor had I even touched my keyboard. The page had simply appeared in front of me.

The warm Teal glow filled me as I turned back to the Amazon page for *Pushout* and ordered my own copy of the book. Apparently, she wasn't letting me off the hook this time.

But then, this was what I'd been praying for all along—a way to have a life that meant something again. Here, at least, was a starting place.

By now I was humble and healed enough to realize that life wasn't ultimately about pulling for me, me, me. Instead, I needed to be here for everyone else as well.

This was just the latest manifestation of what Teal called the Unified Field of Love—that light-filled sea of love just below the surface, where we greet each other not as strangers but as intimate brothers and sisters.

It didn't matter how or where I served others. It could be by talking with school boards, or writing checks, or just giving a little cash to the guy with the bedraggled sign beside the highway ramp. Or even by giving talks about organ donation.

The point was to take action. Each time I did, I found that bright spark of togetherness that unites us all.

I thanked God for the ability to care.

CHAPTER SEVENTEEN

F our months later I was standing on a stage in Dallas, looking out at the crowd of people who'd gathered for the annual conference. I hesitated. Suddenly, I wondered whether I was ready to give this speech. But, of course, it was too late to wonder.

The audience looked at me expectantly.

I clicked on the first slide. A huge image of Teal appeared on the jumbo screen behind me. "First I want to tell you about my daughter," I began. The well-worn urge to cry loomed, but I took a breath, fighting it. How on earth was I going to inspire these people and deliver a pep talk on positivity and transformation? Rather than think about it, I kept going.

The audience was filled with several hundred organ and tissue transplant professionals, people who stood at the edge of death every single day. And they understood innately what it took to come back from the worst crises imaginable. They also reveled in the transformational power of upheaval.

These were my people now.

Out in the audience before me were also some of the very same staff who'd arranged the transplant of Teal's heart, pancreas, kidneys, corneas, her tissues and anything else they could use.

Through some extraordinary slip of fate, I had become the closing keynote speaker at their national conference.

The weight of this opportunity was not lost on me. But in the end, I was still a grieving mother, and they knew it. "I hope you will forgive me if I cry a little as I share my story," I said, as tears began to stream down my face.

Crying on stage. *Not a good look*, my worried mind told me.

A kind woman in front of me immediately stood up and approached the stage with a handkerchief. I smiled and pulled my own out of my suit pocket. "I'm actually prepared," I told her. "I brought my best hankie." We shared a laugh, I blew my nose and wiped my eyes, and so I began.

This is just how it was meant to be, I thought, as I told my story of discovering self-care, and the healing power of crisis to put us right again. I was here, in this small moment, doing what I was meant to do, my vulnerability on full display. Only this time, unlike before, the opportunities seemed to come to me, unbidden.

There would be no pushing, no striving, and no heroics. I would not need to stay up all night, nor would I need to worry myself to sleep. If I simply showed up in good faith every day, ready to follow the instructions, God would take care of the rest. This much I had learned.

I had not yet met Amera, but I wasn't concerned. We lived hours from each other, and our lives were both busy. If it was meant to be, we would meet someday. If it wasn't, we wouldn't. Now I understood that the most powerful truth was simply that this young woman existed, along with Teal's other recipients, and that they all continued to thrive.

Back in my old life, when the Spiritual Marketing Quest was ending, and my relationship was breaking up, and I could smell the burned flesh of destruction all around me, I prayed to God again and again: "Please show me what to do." And always, the answer was the same.

Surrender.

At the time, I couldn't even fathom the answer. Instead, I was mildly indignant. What the hell was 'surrender' supposed to mean? Wasn't there something more God was supposed to tell me?

Like…where were the action items?

In fact, surrendering *was* the entire point. I needed to do nothing more in this life but surrender, again and again and again. This didn't mean surrendering my values, or my boundaries, or my long-held dreams. Instead, I was being called to stop fighting the circumstances of life and all its inevitable lessons. I was being told to embrace reality, just as it was, and to sit with it. To explore it, even.

I'd been called to look turmoil and crisis in the face, and take it apart, one collapse, one death, and one financial transaction at a time. Then it could gently inform me of its purpose.

So, I let the power of Spirit, God, the Universe, Allah, Brahma, Jesus, Devi—and Teal—descend through me and teach me, every day, about the twists and turns of my life. This was the treasure on the other side of all that surrender.

Even if I had to surrender in front of a room full of 300 healthcare workers, all of whom listened intently to me as I spoke and cried. And I shared this wild journey I was on.

Only now would I grow in the ways God intended for me. And only this way, in true service, would my path in this brief life be complete. Simply by offering myself to the world, unvarnished.

The point was no longer to achieve. The point was to do what Teal, herself, used to tell me all the time.

"Just be, Mom," she once said.

I got it now. I really did.

———

I drove toward Sebastopol as golden morning light spread across the rising brown hills that flanked the highway. Oak trees dotted the hills and an occasional cow grazed in the meadow below. My body relaxed slightly as I left the busy world behind and crossed into Sonoma County.

By now my plea was well-worn and familiar. "Honey, if you're listening, please show me what I'm supposed to do next." Then I added a new twist: "If it's the podcast, bless it or block it, okay?"

The idea of a podcast had been on my mind for nearly two years at this point, but I was looking for the right time to launch it, as well as the right message. This, too, would be another way to manifest Teal's spirit and my newfound perspective on life. Yet, like most of my work these days, I felt so tentative and raw, it was hard to get going.

I was doing something my friend Jon called the Bless It or Block It prayer, and it was a gorgeously unscientific way to make decisions. You simply asked Spirit, your angels, or whomever was guiding you at the moment, to give you a definitive sign, pro or con, about what to do next.

The Teal presence swelled up and a small burst of laughter rippled through me. She would show me. That much I knew.

Each time I began the podcast project, I hesitated again. But this was the way of grief, full of false fits and starts, and so laced with uncertainty. So far I had a musical intro for the show that a friend helped me put together, but that was all.

A little while later I stepped up to the counter in my favorite tea shop in Sebastopol and ordered my usual house chai and a muffin. As I stood there, I noticed a tall blonde woman standing outside the doors of the café. She was talking to Magick, the resident psychic.

I looked at her. Then I looked again. She seemed vaguely familiar. At that moment, she gazed back at me and smiled broadly. Then she waved.

It was Michaela, a local shaman who had worked with both Teal and I in the month before her death. Then I'd lain on her table while she snipped various energetic cords, and with the shake of a rattle and the sprinkle of a mysterious water, dispelled the karmic bond that had held me fast to my former lover Whit.

I couldn't possibly explain what had just happened. Yet on that day, I left feeling remarkably better.

Within moments, Michaela was seated in the armchair next to me as we spontaneously shared a cup of tea. I began telling her about connecting with Amera and my talks in the organ procurement world. Together, we pondered the connection between bodies and souls as organs and tissues are transferred.

Every so often, Michaela's eyes would close slightly and she'd tip her head. "I'm getting something," she would say, as she began to bring in a message from her guides. It struck me now what Teal and I had heard from the restaurant lecturer the night of her collapse that shamans traveled between worlds, conveying messages from the other side.

Now Michaela looked up. "Teal is all over me right now," she remarked, as she began to repeat the words in her head.

When my heart stopped, I was shocked. I couldn't believe it. My soul was ready to go, but I was not aware that my heart had a different trajectory. Michaela began.

Immediately I thought of the first ethereal encounter I had with Teal, just after her collapse, when her spirit visited me in a San Francisco hotel room. At the time she told me she was *trying to reconcile her heart and her soul.* This was not something I'd shared with Michaela. Or anyone.

Michaela continued, her eyes closed.

There's a way in which when I was young I didn't understand the pain that my heart was in. And I didn't know I could sustain it. And yet, my heart's journey was really to impart information from another dimensional aspect so people could hear the wisdom of my heart and other hearts. I was not capable of doing that psychologically in the body that I had, and with the personality that I had. I wasn't evolved enough to understand that in order to heal the heart, I had to experience what the heart was harboring.

This all seemed so very true. Teal's heart was so fragile and yet so full at the same time. I thought about her therapist telling me after her death that Teal's biggest concern wasn't love, or anxiety, or even fear. It was simply how to tolerate the very intensity of life.

And I thought of Teal's quiet, and sometimes not so quiet, empathy.

"You can't just talk to people like that!" she would storm at me if I was rude to anyone. "What were you thinking?"

Then I remembered her insistence that I substantially over tip every waitperson who served us. "You have no idea what it's like," she'd assure me, remembering her own days waiting tables.

Michaela and I sat in silence for a minute, and it occurred to me that this, right here and right now, was the podcast. In it would be all that I had learned from Teal since her death. It would, in fact, be her legacy.

"I don't know about you, but I feel fantastic," Michaela commented as we both got up to leave a little while later. "I came in here with things on my mind, but all that energy…it was terrific!"

I agreed completely. Something magical had just happened in our hour together; something sweet and serene and perfect.

If I needed more confirmation, it arrived a few moments later as I drove away. I turned on the car stereo, pushed the button to play my iPod on Shuffle and in came Teal's voice, an a cappella arrangement of her own layered harmonies.

"Bum bum ba bum, bum ba bum, bum ba bum… Wade in the water… Wade in the water, childre …"

It was the theme music I'd recorded for the podcast.

I drove home in bliss that afternoon. With each day that passed, Teal's death began to make more and more sense. And my path was becoming clearer and clearer.

There was, indeed, a larger purpose. Together, we would heal people in a number of ways—essays, a book. A podcast. And so together, once again, we fulfilled God's plan for us.

We were moving ahead, in perfect sync.

Deborah, Luke and I drove toward Berkeley as small raindrops began to scatter across the windshield. The sky had been getting progressively darker and a steady rain threatened. Which really would have been fine, except that we were heading for our wedding.

"We'll be having the reception inside, you know," Deborah remarked.

"Yeah," I agreed.

Luke piped up from the back seat. "Don't worry about it," he said. "It'll be fine."

That was true, of course, because at this point it hardly mattered whether iced tea and sangria would be served inside or out. A little more than two years after meeting, we were getting married.

Married!

The long slog back to my true identity was reaching its next satisfying conclusion, and I was marrying the love of my life.

I looked over at Deborah and took her hand. How had I gotten so fortunate to find this strong, vibrant, deeply caring woman? How had I been so fortunate that God listened to my singular request in the darkness…for the woman who was my equal, my true mate?

On the other hand, maybe it wasn't up to me at all. Maybe the shoes of this relationship had been neatly placed next to my bed all along, and one day I was finally ready to put them on.

We married that morning in a soaring stone building, a 1930s California Gothic designed by the famed architect Julia Morgan. As we sat in our small gold chairs, the ceremony unfolded around us, and we could feel the perfect rightness of this moment. Words were spoken and songs were sung, and our minister, a radiant, bald Black lesbian named Reverend Jacqueline, filled the room with her humor, her joy, and her own stunning incandescence.

"Oh happy *DAY!*" she exulted as the ceremony began, and everyone in the room cheered.

When it came time for the Reverend to ask us if it was our intention to marry, a sudden, direct ray of sun broke through the clouds and poured into the very spot where we stood. The room gave a gasp, and then a sigh of delight.

And as we began our vows, I suddenly saw how far I had come from the early days of my own repression. Then my lesbianism had been like a dream, something I assumed I would never actually get to live, even though I longed for it with all my heart.

Back then, I had lived in a prison of my own making. It was a place I assumed I deserved to be. But now, right here, in the radiant sunlight of the Berkeley City Club, surrounded by people who loved us, it was finally, entirely, jubilantly safe to be me.

A moment later, Reverend Jacqueline proudly pronounced us legally married spouses for life, and the crowd spontaneously stood up and cheered. We kissed and they cheered once more. Then we walked down the aisle as "The Lover's Waltz" played on. We were officially spouses for life.

Now I understood. Love doesn't just happen because you find the right person.

It happens when you find the right you.

CHAPTER EIGHTEEN

Deborah and I sat in traffic at an always-congested spot called The Maze. Ahead of us was the Bay Bridge and San Francisco, and in the distance, the glittering bay. As usual, we were in standstill traffic. I sank down into my seat as Deborah inched the car along, and I closed my eyes. This was the last thing I needed right now.

I was filled with so many swirling emotions—fear, longing, grief, and joy. And now frustration was added to the list. We were going to be late to meet Amera and her mother. But then it had been three years since I'd gotten Amera's letter. So, what was another half hour?

"I can't believe this," I grumbled, eyes snapping open. "Look at this!"

Deborah said nothing. Glancing over at me, she took my hand and gave it a squeeze. Leaning back, I tried to relax. Suddenly, the tension in my body gave way and I began to understand. There was nothing to worry about here—nothing at all. These people were eternally grateful to us, as we were eternally grateful to them. And being late because of traffic would not blow everything to hell.

Still, I could not help the pounding in my chest, and the

sheer anticipation of the entire thing. I just wanted to get there. To finally meet Amera. To see, and feel, what had been wrought. And to be just one inch closer, somehow, to my daughter.

In the days leading up to our meeting, my motherly instincts had kicked in through a series of messages to Amera. *It'll probably be cold on Ocean Beach,* I wrote to her. *Don't forget your layers.*

Of course, it hadn't occurred to me that Amera, a grown woman and a lifelong Californian, had been on more chilly beaches than I had.

She took no offense, and gamely assured me she'd already packed a hat and gloves. Amera also wrote this:

I've also been wondering if Teal's father and brother know that we are meeting? I would love to meet both of them as well if that is something that they want.

I let her know that Larry and Luke did indeed know we were meeting, and they were happy to hear it. And they were still 3,000 miles away, which meant that I was doing the family representing for now.

Finally, after another hour of working our way through San Francisco traffic, Deborah and I arrived at the beach. We pulled up and parked. We looked at each other and locked hands as we stepped out on the sea wall.

Ocean Beach spread out before us, washed by the Pacific. It was a stunning day, and the blue skies were full of promise. It was here nearly five years earlier that Larry, Luke and I stood in the same frigid water, scattering Teal's ashes, releasing what was left of her body into the wind and the sea. And now here we were—specifically because Amera had requested it.

"I would love to meet you in the place where you scattered Teal's remains," she'd said, which endeared her to me forever.

"Do you see them?" Deborah asked me, as we scanned the wide-open beach before us.

I surveyed the many, far away figures dotting the shoreline, looking for Amera and her mother, Debi. They could have been any of the people before us, really. But then, maybe that was the point.

Deborah and I walked uncertainly down onto the sand and glanced around. I took off my sandals, and carrying them in my hand, began to meander along, hoping to find them.

Then suddenly there they were, walking toward us, waving. The two were unmistakable: a taller, younger woman, and beside her, her mother, a shorter woman walking across the sand with a cane.

Amera was lovely, with long blonde hair and an easy smile. She had the air of the young and insouciant. Happy, relaxed, carefree. And taller than I expected. Despite all she had suffered, an essential peace still shone through Amera, even at a distance.

By now, her body had owned and integrated Teal's organs for five full years. They had literally become her, as each cell in her body replaced itself again and again.

Once more I was reminded that Teal, the five-foot-six brunette with the beautiful singing voice, the irresistible laugh, the tiny nose ring, and the side-swept bangs, no longer existed. Yet, the real Teal—the great glowing spiritual presence she had become—was far bigger than her body, her personality or even her transplanted organs. And perhaps she had joined us as well for our meeting.

One thing I knew for sure. Teal's gift was to become a healer of all hearts, just as she had healed mine and Amera's. We were merely among the first fortunate recipients.

"Amera," I said as I approached her, and we dissolved into an enormous hug.

Tears overtook both of us, and we held that hug for a long, long time. Together we could feel our profound connection, and our ever-unfolding gratitude. For life. For generosity. And for our shared humanity.

I was reluctant to let go of that hug, but finally I did. Now I was beginning to understand that helping to save Amera's life would be one of the things I was most proud of in this lifetime. Perhaps it was one of the few things that really mattered.

Alongside Amera stood her mother, Debi, a pretty, petite, dark-haired woman with a huge smile. She immediately struck me as one of the more positive people I'd ever met. Somehow she exuded it even as we began to shake hands. Then we both dissolved into a massive, teary, mother-to-mother hug.

In an instant, I could feel all she had been through—the all-night hospital marathons, the terrifying medical bills. The doctor consults, the bad diagnoses, the moments and hours of tension and confusion about what to do next.

And the ever-present fear she'd lived with for eight years, that this gorgeous young woman in front of us could die at any moment. Apparently, she had endured all of this as a single mother with a disability, while raising two other children as well. I knew I was in the presence of real strength.

Debi had carried Amera through all of it, refusing to leave her side for even a moment. She was obviously a formidable woman. And yet, here she was, smiling up at me. Kind, solid. A truly good soul. I could feel it.

We stood chatting for a moment, then another. Then finally, slowly, we began to wander up the beach. It was not until several minutes later that I suddenly realized I'd lost my shoes.

"Jesus," I said in dismay, color flooding my face.

"Ah, don't worry about it," said Debi with an easy chuckle. "You're just rolling like me." Then we both laughed.

"Okay, let's fan out," she suggested. Debi was clearly used to solving problems.

The four of us combed the beach in a human chain, back-tracking for several moments, until we finally found the missing Birkenstocks.

I picked them up with a twinge of embarrassment. Still, I needn't have been abashed—not with these two. They were the sort of people who would never ever judge me. I could already feel that.

We sat down to dinner at a nearby restaurant a little while later, and suddenly I felt nervous. Shy, really. Perhaps it was the overwhelm of the moment, or just the raw reality that sitting across from the table from me was a relative stranger who now carried my daughter's cells, tissues, muscles. Her DNA.

Yet, she now also carried the tiniest bit of my own DNA, along with Larry's and an untold number of our ancestors. Even though Amera's cells would replicate again and again for the rest of her life, that little corner of her body would always have Teal's unique imprint.

I ordered a glass of wine.

Eventually, after some small talk, we got down to business. Amera and Debi told us their story. Since Teal's death, it had been hard for me to grasp the full significance of the transplants. But as they shared what they'd been through—the surgeries, the problems, the backtracking, the near-death moments—I began to understand more and more how crucial Teal's organs were.

As we sat and talked, the similarities kept popping up again and again. For one thing, Amera's sensitivity was absolute. As she spoke of her emerging career as a cardio stenographer, she was moved to tears describing her patients' suffering. She, too, felt everyone around her with deep compassion. Just like Teal.

Like Teal, Amera had also chosen a career that would help people heal. She was even completing her studies at San Francisco's City College, the very same place Teal was to begin attending classes the day after her collapse.

The source of Amera's congestive heart failure also remained unknown—just like the exact cause of Teal's cardiac arrests. Amera even longed to travel the world, as Teal once had. In the past five years, she, too, had begun exploring overseas, hitting a number of the same countries Teal, herself, had been to.

But then Amera said something that really made her kinship with my daughter clear.

"I want to help you with your talks someday," she offered. "But not until I make something of myself." Her simple modesty blew me away. That, too, was just like Teal, who was never one to crave the spotlight.

But now as we sat there, another thought struck me. Perhaps Amera wasn't ready to give talks with me, but maybe her mother could instead.

Debi was warm, accessible, and funny. She could tell a good story. Sitting across the table from me, she radiated a certain, very specific type of energy—a front of the room, onstage energy. Just like me.

So far, I knew little about the rest of Debi's life, except that she'd been a high-level dental assistant for decades. And that she was looking for her next act. She was also clearly a people person, one who'd been dealing with the public for decades.

It was possible that Debi could be the sort of speaker audiences would really love. If she wanted to go there. Instantly, I knew I could teach her to become a speaker—potentially an excellent speaker. After all, I'd spent part of my last decade teaching people to package their message and deliver it on stage.

For a moment, as I ate my dinner, I considered how powerful it would be for Debi and I to share our story with audiences together. She asked me about the talks I'd been giving, and she listened attentively as I described them.

"How do you even do that?" Debi had wondered aloud. And she posited that speaking would be terrifying to her. "I'd have to wear a diaper," she laughed.

Shaking my head, I pushed all thoughts of speaking with Debi out of my mind. *Here I go again,* I thought to myself, *getting way ahead of myself.* Though we'd exchanged numbers and promised to keep in touch, the last thing I wanted was to be pushy and striving. Despite the signals that were currently inundating my brain.

After dinner, I had something to share with Debi and Amera. I'd brought along my laptop, cued up to play a video of

Teal singing the civil rights anthem "A Change Is Gonna Come." It was filmed in her friend Nacho's living room in the Mission district of San Francisco. I offered to play it for them, and they eagerly agreed.

We went downstairs to the lobby of the building, and I set the laptop up on a nearby counter. I started the video, and we all watched silently.

In the clip, Teal is her free-spirited self, as relaxed, soulful, and easy as I'd ever seen her. She wears a simple gray t-shirt, a leather thong around her neck and her travel guitar in hand. Her beautiful honey colored hair hangs around her face in thick strands, and her side-swept bangs brush her eyelashes.

She is silent for a moment as she waits to begin her song. Then Nacho, playing the guitar beside her, strums a single chord. She gives the smile of someone who truly loves to sing, and she lets loose the first line, about being born by a river.

Teal's rich, clear voice soars in a way that is both strong and tender. It is obvious how much she feels as she sings. Sam Cooke wrote the song back at the height of the Civil Rights Movement, all about justice and injustice, and hope, and the building of a bridge between people. It expresses everything Teal stood for in her short life.

Silently, we watch Teal croon the words, her eyes closed.

Her song is strong and true, her phrasing beautiful. She giggles as Nacho attempts a rough scat on the bridge, and she beams at him and picks up the humming encouragingly when he falters. Moments later, as the song ends, Teal ends with a final crooned note and a laugh of pure joy. It is a stunning, simple performance.

When the video finished, I turned it off and we were all quiet for a moment. "I know her," Amera finally said. Her voice was filled with wonder.

Amera knew her. Here was confirmation of everything I had suspected for so long.

For if there was ever a reason for one young woman to

become deathly ill for eight years, and for another to simply drop dead—both from unexplained, mysterious causes—this had to be it.

There was no denying these two shared a certain karma, just as all do who share transplanted organs. They danced, and continue to dance, in a cosmic union neither could have ever predicted or even fully understood.

For me, this was simply another example of the intense and forgiving Grace of the Universe. A Universe that takes away just as breathtakingly as it provides, again and again. Each time it does, we have the chance to rise up and be reborn. But that only happens if we allow it.

This much I had learned from Teal's death.

As it turned out, Amera and Debi had a gift for me as well that night. Moments after I closed my laptop, I was hunkered down in the backseat of their car, the ends of a stethoscope plugged into my ears.

Amera had borrowed the stethoscope from a nurse she knew just so I could hear Teal's heartbeat before the night ended. I hadn't actually heard her heartbeat since she was in utero, back when I was lying on the obstetrician's table. But sitting there in the car, I smiled as I listened to that heartbeat once again.

It filled me with a sense I can only describe as completion. Here was Teal. Again.

Here was the gift, quiet and true. For within every crisis there is possibility. Within the darkest grief there are hollows of love. And within the very texture of life, there is hope. I knew that now with all my heart.

I walked away that night, certain that my path with Amera and Debi had only just begun.

CHAPTER NINETEEN

The morning after we met on the beach, I woke up thinking about Debi. I couldn't shake the feeling that we were supposed to be speaking together. A little while later, I texted her, telling her how happy I was that we met. *What a great night it was,* I wrote.

Immediately Debi responded in kind. At that moment, she said, she was waiting for her daughter at her cardiologist's office in San Francisco.

She's wonderful and I'm so blessed to have her at all, let alone still have her. I hope we can always stay in touch.

Then, a few moments later, Debi sent this text: *If you want me to come on stage and talk from my end about all of this, I will get over my fear of speaking just for that... Seriously, I will have to wear a diaper.*

I smiled to myself. I was pretty sure she wouldn't need a diaper at all.

As luck would have it, our breakout moment arrived only a few weeks later. A meeting planner called wondering if I might speak to a conference of 300 transplant nurses in Minneapolis. The gig was only a few months away. Immediately, I wanted to pitch the idea of Debi appearing on stage with me, but I held off on bringing it up with the planner.

Better, I thought, to see whether Debi seriously wanted to appear on stage first. After some false starts and a lot of encouragement from her boss and coworkers at the dental office where she worked, she agreed a few days later. So we set to work.

Debi's first job was to write out a rough draft of her half of the story, and then practice reading it into a voice recording app. She emailed me one week later.

I've been recording myself, wow, wow. I sure hope I get better really soon.

She attached the first draft of her talk. It was a high-velocity waterfall of notes, a collage of intense experiences all piled on top of one another. The document was single spaced and several pages long.

I'm no writer, she added in her email. Perhaps not, but she had definitely captured the essence of her story.

We agreed that I would come up to Debi's house in the foothills of the Sierras, where she lived with her fiancé Chuck, and we would hash out the flow of her speech together. Then I could coach her live on delivery. She was remarkably game.

Debi messaged me a little while later. *I always feel better when we talk. I hope that's true for you too.* It was. We were quickly discovering we had amazing friend chemistry. And now, an extraordinary shared history, as well.

One week later, I found myself driving past late fall cornfields being scavenged by crows and tidy country homes with pickups in the driveway. I was on my way to Debi's. Eventually I found my way to their driveway. I pulled up behind a toy hauler and parked. Their house was small, trim, and neat with what appeared to be a big backyard.

I rang the doorbell and a moment later, there stood Debi, looking intense and a little smaller than I remembered her. A huge smile broke across her face. "Hey!" she said, reaching for a hug.

Chuck's towering figure filled the doorway behind her. "You must be Suzanne!" he said, his face lit with a huge smile. We went in for a hug, as well.

Debi and I sat at her kitchen table and talked about a million things. Eventually, we circled around to our talk, now less than a month away. When it was time to work, we walked to the toy hauler in the driveway, where there was room to spread out.

Propped up on the queen-sized bed in the corner, I madly typed notes on my laptop while Debi paced back and forth recounting details of their story. More and more bits and pieces kept emerging.

"Did I tell you about the little man I saw that night in the hospital?" Debi asked.

"Tell me," I said.

On that night, back at the beginning of Amera's illness, it was entirely possible she would die. Her heart was now failing dramatically and nothing seemed able to bring it under control. A massive dose of antibiotics was administered. It became a wait-and-see situation.

Debi's thoughts were a jumble of negative emotions that night, so while Amera slept, she took a walk through the hospital to calm herself.

The place was quiet, the hallways dark. Debi saw a gymnasium at the end of an empty corridor and wandered toward it curiously. She ducked her head inside and looked around. When she stepped back into the hallway, a shrunken old man with a walker and an oxygen tank was sitting on a bench in front of her.

He hadn't been there seconds earlier. Immediately, Debi glanced up and down the hallway, wondering where he'd come from.

The old man looked at her kindly and suddenly Debi found herself crying. In a soothing voice he told her, "Everything's going to be okay." She took him in with his bald head and his gentle demeanor. It struck her that he had the air of someone who'd lived a long time and knew things. As Debi studied his face, something shifted for her.

"I'm not the kind of person who ever believed that Amera was going to die," she later recalled. "At first, I got sucked into those thoughts a little. But then, as I stood there talking to the old man, I thought, *oh no, this ain't taking me down.*"

A new resolve filled Debi as she hurried back upstairs to Amera. By the time she reached Amera's room, her daughter had woken up and she was now in tears. Amera was seriously scared.

Debi took her daughter's hand and leaned forward intently. She looked her daughter right in the eye. "Honey," she said with emphasis, "we are not going to cry about this anymore. You are going to get better. We're going to laugh again, and love the people we love, and things are going to be all right."

Amera looked up at her mother, her young, innocent face still awash with fear. "Okay, Mom," she said in a little girl voice. Desperately, she wanted to believe her mother.

As Debi told me this story, I typed as fast I could, trying to get it all down. The floodgates had now officially opened. I just prayed I could keep up.

Debi stopped pacing for a moment and looked at me. "Hey, did I tell you the part about Amera glowing?"

That stopped me cold, and I looked up from my laptop. This was the first I'd heard of this. "What about glowing?"

"I didn't tell you this already? I can't believe it." Debi shook her head. Then she paused and looked at me. "Okay, so on the day of the transplant, I went in to see Amera about an hour after the she got her heart. She was stabilizing in Recovery before going back in for the kidney. And when I walked in the room…" Her voice trailed off, and then her voice cracked slightly. "Suzanne, her entire body was glowing. There was like…this golden glow."

Debi paused thoughtfully, as if she could see it all over again. A look of reverence lit her face. "It was radiating all around her body, and it was as bright as a pair of headlights. It lasted the entire time I was there. I couldn't take my eyes off her."

I looked at Debi, listening.

"I thought I was going crazy," she continued, "but my sister Darla walked in then, and she turned to me and said, 'Hey, she's glowing.'"

I knew that sparkling, effervescent glow. It was my daughter.

Debi and I were silent for a moment, and now the tears that had been threatening all afternoon began to pour down my face in earnest. Sooner or later I knew Teal's essence was going to show up in this story, and here it was, loud and clear. I closed my eyes and leaned my head back against the wall as I sobbed.

I gave myself a few moments to just fall apart as Debi moved in for a hug. We held on to each other, two moms who'd truly seen it all.

"That was Teal," I blubbered into her shoulder.

"Yeah," Debi agreed, as she, too, began to cry. "I know."

The two of us continued to have a cry together. As we did nearly every time we met. Finally, I blew my nose once more and pulled myself together.

"Jesus," I finally said, blowing my nose. "You okay?" I asked her and she nodded. I handed her a tissue from a nearby box.

"Yep," Debi said with a laugh, drying her tears. "This is just…so big…."

My mind reveled in this new glorious detail. *Teal's heart made Amera glow.* It was stunning. And I knew it was true.

As long as Amera walked this earth, Teal would as well in some tiny way. Her great, glowing, love-filled energy—her very sweetest part—would live on and on. Amera was amazing now, healthy, thriving, and doing good things in the world. Yet, now there was something else, as well.

As Debi put it, she had "a touch of Teal."

CHAPTER TWENTY

B y now, I'd become accustomed to the gentle creep of guided messages that met me in the early light of the morning. It was a little like checking my emails, only I did it while lying in bed with my eyes closed.

On this particular morning the clear voice of Spirit sang through my head. *It's time to start the group.*

A Facebook group? I wondered to myself. The confirmation was swift and immediate.

Yes, a Facebook group. Like the book I was now working on, it was to be called Self-Care for Extremely Busy Women.

An avalanche of instructions came cascading through my consciousness, a waterfall of purpose with layer upon layer of insights. I wasn't sure who the sender was, and it didn't even matter—the imperative was clear. This was to be a healing group for all kinds of women who need encouragement and support around self-care.

I groped for the notebook that was usually on my bedside table, but it wasn't there. Instead, my fingers closed around a discarded envelope. Ripping it apart, I began scribbling notes as I felt them pour through me.

A healing place for women.
Simply lead by being—there is no 'work' here.
Opening the door for them to come flooding in.

The vision was compelling. It would be a place for women to relax. For them to ask what they needed to ask and say what they needed to say. It was to be an intimate group where we could all support each other to get what we needed in our lives. And it would be filled with loving kindness.

We would be a broad panoply of women from all over the world. And we would hang out together in the Unified Field of Love. Collectively, we would all heal each other.

Spirit wrapped up the cavalcade of information on this note: *You will know when the time is right.*

As usual my guides were being maddeningly unclear, yet perfectly clear at the same time. I smiled at my hubris. Of course, I was trying to figure all of this out in advance. Had I learned nothing?

Already, I could feel the larger truth. This group would test the very limits of my ability to lead. Yet, there was no blueprint, just as there were no instructions. I would simply have to learn by doing.

I was suddenly filled with a stab of fear. What if I blew it? What if I failed Teal's mission for us?

What if I ended up leading no one? What if her legacy became nothing more than a dusty, forgotten memory? What if the group failed to attract...anyone?

I felt Spirit smile through me, amused at the thrashings of my small human mind. Again, the larger truth beamed. Ultimately, this group would be more important than the book. And it well might be the truest expression of my light leadership.

If, of course, I wanted to rise to the occasion.

I wanted to! I wanted to! Oh, yes, I did.

Now, five and a half years after Teal's death, my grief had given way to a clear-eyed awareness about my place in the world.

I'd stopped crying and become humbler. My life was far simpler, my addictive behaviors were in check, and I was much, much happier. I made less money, yet I needed less money. And my days moved in a sweet and perfect harmony.

For the first time since…well, ever possibly…I felt entirely right in my skin. I'd finally learned how to love and take care of myself, and to ask for help when I needed it. Just as I'd learned to set boundaries and stop attracting needy, crazy people into my life.

But could I really pull this group thing off? Spirit's vision seemed huge, and I was uncertain. Silently, I invoked Teal. *Show me that you're with me on this*, I asked.

Not surprisingly, Teal put in an appearance the very next day, courtesy of our friend Wendy. Deborah and I sang with Wendy in a Unitarian church choir in Oakland, and occasionally she came over to rehearse.

The first time she came to the house, Wendy had sensed what she called a "young, intense spirit" lingering by us, as we stood around our piano, singing. Wendy was not a professional medium or a psychic. (She was actually a piano and voice teacher.) Yet picking up spiritual energy had always been easy for her. So we mused that the young spirit Wendy sensed around us could be Teal.

Since she, too, had once been a singer, perhaps she wanted to join the party.

The next time we heard from Teal, Deborah, Wendy, and I were on our way to a rehearsal together, and Wendy was gazing out the window in the back seat as I drove along the highway. Suddenly she spoke up from the back.

"Hey," she said, "I've got Teal outside my window, and she's holding out a book."

After a pause, Wendy continued evenly, "She says this book is very important." Though Wendy had no idea what I was working on at the moment, there was no question in my mind which book she was referring to. I had just finished the final draft of a book about self-care, and I'd attracted a publisher. The book deal had been signed a few months earlier.

The image of Teal holding out a glowing, open book had appeared to me in a number of dreams and meditations over the last few years. It was an image I already knew well. Wendy continued, "She also says to be careful around Green. Do you know someone named Green?"

I sighed. Green was a backup singer in an R&B band I now sang with. I had been rude to her recently after she was late to a rehearsal. Immediately, I felt a pang of guilt, and I knew I owed Green an apology. Why did I have to be such a bull in a china shop?

I wasn't surprised that Teal picked up my transgression from the afterlife. It was exactly the sort of thing she would have remarked on when she was alive.

Now, here I was several weeks later getting this massive download about the Facebook group. Although I'd been thinking about starting such a group, a new urgency took hold as this flood of notes moved through me, and its true purpose became clear.

The time for the group was now.

As I scribbled in the early light that morning, I began to beat myself up. Why had I waited to start the group? I could have had this up for at least a few months already, I chided myself.

I felt the sludge of my age-old resistance to my most important projects. A moldy sense of shame mixed with fear that descended when it was time to put myself out there most vulnerably. I'd had this feeling as long as I could remember. And here it was again.

Sighing, I did my best to shake off my doubts. It was time to start the group. I had to begin now, no matter how scared I was.

As if on cue, Wendy arrived to rehearse with me the next day. When I let her in, she smiled. "Just heard from Teal a minute ago," she said, taking off her coat.

"Not sure what this means, but she said 'Don't worry, Mom. I can wait.'" I smiled at the rightness of her words.

As if I needed another dose of confirmation, Debi called me a few days later. We'd recently given our first talk together about the organ donation experience, and it was a success. In fact, we were now preparing to give another talk. But that's not where our conversation began.

"Hey, so Teal gave me a message!" she exclaimed with her usual enthusiasm. By now even Debi was being visited by Teal's sparkling essence. This visit happened while she was driving. "I'm not sure what it meant but I heard her say, 'Women...help women.'" Debi paused. "I got the clear sense that the purpose was self-care."

A chill ran down my spine. Here was the Facebook group again.

Message. Fully. Received.

CHAPTER TWENTY-ONE

The Self-Care Group for Extremely Busy Women began quietly. First a few hundred of my stalwart readers joined. Then a few hundred more women found it by searching for 'self-care' in Facebook's Groups section. In fits and starts the group began to grow.

Initially, I posted ideas about flavoring your water, or painless sit ups, or getting better sleep, thinking of myself as a benevolent self-care overlord. Yet, none of these posts really got much traction. I realized that no one really cared what I actually thought about these matters. And honestly, it wasn't my sweet spot. Emotional self-care was more my jam.

So my path became clearer. I wasn't ever going to be one of willowy influencers with the long honey locks, ideas for date night with the hubs, keto smoothies, and a half-million followers. If I was going to do this group honestly, it wasn't going to be about me at all.

Instead, it was going to be about the group and the care and feeding of *their* hearts and souls. By now, I was clear that this is what mattered to me about most. So I switched tracks. What really got the group going, I discovered, was asking questions.

Not only did I ask questions now, but I also quickly learned to tune in to Teal's energy each time before I did so. Or I felt into my gut—what would I *like* to ask in that moment? And the answer always swam right up.

What could you let go of that would make life easier?
Who do you need to ask for help?
What do you need right now?
What are you tolerating?
The answers in those first few years were predictable.
I need to lose fifty pounds.
I need to tell my boss I can't work on the weekends.
I need to get the kids to do the dishes.
I need a vacation!

The group stayed focused on pure self-care, with the occasional shot of girl talk as members chatted about whether that vacation should be in Florida or New England, and where to find a really efficient, small, washable purse. The mood was convivial, and it had the air of a Sunday afternoon tea party among women who'd just met.

It was sweet.

The group grew as friends referred friends, and Facebook occasionally recommended the group. Almost two years after it started, we had 10,000 members. I still wasn't sure exactly how this had happened, and I marveled at it.

Yet far more growth—eye-popping, explosive growth—was just ahead. For which, I was definitely not prepared.

It began on a February morning in 2021, as the COVID-19 pandemic was peaking and cresting. More than half a million had died from the virus at this point, and COVID was now the leading cause of death in the United States. I reached for my phone one morning and clicked into the Facebook group. I glanced at the Member Request area, as I always did, expecting to see maybe twenty or thirty new ones.

There were 2,700.

Twenty-seven hundred.

I sat up, blinking, not quite sure I'd read that right. Immediately I went in to look, suspecting that the group had been hacked. Or that some kind of tech weirdness had suddenly made the same person request membership 2,700 times. But no. There really were 2,700 requests, all apparently from legitimate would-be members.

And these were just the ones who showed up while I slept.

Adrenaline rushed through my body as I hurried from the bedroom. Snapping open my laptop, I struggled to understand what had happened. Each person who wanted to join the group was asked some questions, including *How did you hear about us?* I scanned the responses.

Person after person said the same thing—Facebook had recommended the group.

Apparently, overnight, my self-care group had suddenly hit Facebook big time. Still in my pajamas, I started admitting members like mad. And I didn't stop for hours.

The next day I woke up to another 1,800 requests. There were 3,600 the day after that, and the pace just continued. One morning a few weeks later, I actually woke up to more than 5,400 requests.

It was as if the only person who was sleeping at night was me. Everybody else was busy cruising Facebook, looking for self-care groups to join. And the push for membership carried on all day, every day. Sometimes there were so many people trying to join at one time that the system would get backed up, hiccupping at me furiously.

The requests kept pouring in as February slid into March. LaTisha from Illinois, Mary from Omaha, Denise from Anchorage, Priya from Bangalore—they all wanted in. As did an entire crew of women from a research station in Antarctica. Within a few weeks we'd admitted 10,000 new members and refused another 12,000, mostly because they were men or they didn't answer the question asking if they agreed to the rules.

I quickly discovered I couldn't possibly process all these requests myself. Yet, I couldn't just hit the 'Admit All' button either. Someone needed to vet each of these would-be members to keep the tenderness, the vulnerability—the integrity of the group together. For Facebook was awash with fake profiles and scammers who liked to infiltrate groups like this. I'd also offered incoming members my free self-care materials, so I needed to collect their email addresses and move them into my system as well.

My assistant Danielle, as game as she was, could only do so much. As could I. We quickly came to realize no human being could process more than 100 to 150 of these requests per hour, so no matter how many hours we put in admitting people, there were always another 5,000 to 10,000 women waiting to join.

I was afraid that if I didn't stay on top of the requests, the firehose would slow to a trickle and Facebook would stop recommending the group. I hired a team of freelance group administrators, mostly based in Manilla. They were a gung-ho team who genuinely loved the group, some of them processing more than 150 requests an hour.

Meanwhile, the action on the discussion board exploded. At any given time, the entire group was active in the group— 20,000 and then 30,000 women. So we went from having twenty-five posts per day to hundreds, which then attracted thousands of comments. All of which needed to be moderated to make sure no one was self-promoting or posting videos or spreading misinformation. Or being a jerk.

I skimped on this part, figuring my focus should be on admitting people. The group would take care of itself, I hoped. Meanwhile the group made a deep, spontaneous dive together into the real nitty gritty of life.

As more and more women poured in, the posts became far more intense, revealing the very big, very real issues these women had in their lives. Women wrote about feeling sexually ignored by their husbands, while others realized their relationships were toxic, or that they were being verbally abused. Still others talked about how they couldn't set boundaries around intrusive parents or their difficult children. And some just needed to blow some steam, after which they usually wrote something like *Thanks for letting me rant…I needed that.*

Again and again, the group showed up for each other, showering these suffering strangers with virtual love and support. A lot of them had been there, done that, and had practical wisdom to share. The level of genuine caring that infused the group was stunning. For which I thanked God for. Because by now I realized I was seriously in over my head. Especially when a few women posted about feeling suicidal. Fortunately, there were mental health professionals in the group who steered them toward help every single time. By now I'd realized I needed to keep the suicide hotline number visible in the group's announcements.

It was as if we all needed this refuge from the dangerous, infectious, angry world that was exploding right outside our doors. In less than a year, millions had died from the virus around the world, while millions had marched demanding social justice for the killing of George Floyd, Breonna Taylor and so many others.

California was burning up with the worst wildfires on record, while other states suffered catastrophic floods again and again. And one day, we watched an insurrection on the US capital on our television—a sight I never could have expected to see in a million years.

Meanwhile, all the trusty staples of our daily lives, from my R&B band to the local library and our favorite bakery, closed down around us. Even the grocery store became a fraught and uncertain place. We stayed home day after day, night after night, feeling more and more uneasy about our lives. It was pretty clear that nothing would ever be the same again.

So here we were, clinging to a virtual group of strangers.

Here we found we could give and receive the solace we so badly needed.

Frontline workers in the group posted about being burned out as they watched their patients die. While others were scared, admitting they needed to lose two hundred pounds, or quit smoking, or leave their broken marriages. A remarkable number of women posted about how hard it was to make friends, and they wondered why. The level of vulnerability and trust seemed to grow every day.

Together we held space for the woman whose daughter was shot in the head by a stray bullet and had to completely relearn everything, beginning with how to walk. And for the woman dying from terminal cancer who described how her perspective shifted after her diagnosis.

I have lived a life believing self-care was for wimps, she wrote. *I carried the weight of my world on my shoulders proudly. An abusive husband. Raising a special needs child for the most part alone. A close family member with an addiction. Keeping a small business afloat through a recession and eventual single parenthood. I literally never realized what it felt like to not live with the stress of an abusive spouse until he went to federal prison. And it has killed me.*

I write this not for sympathy, but to tell you emphatically: you matter. Take a bath. Buy bath bombs. Tell your kids that you're taking two hours for yourself and don't feel guilty about it. Eat healthy. And eat chocolate. Love the people who deserve your love. Forgive yourself. Accept God's grace. Buy some flowers. And don't wait until someone tells you your time is up.

Every single member now subscribed to an unspoken rule that had somehow magically slid into place. We needed to carry each other through this vast wasteland that had become our lives.

And we needed to do it with loving grace.

All this time, I'd naively assumed that such loving kindness would simply carry on. That I could keep my focus on admitting members, and the group's content would take care of itself. Even as the group pushed 40,000.

Sure, they'd be a little conflict here and there, but I could handle it, right? Or so went my uninformed thinking. I had no idea just how volatile a group like this could be. Or that serious trouble could start at night while I was asleep. In my mind, it was just a happy little self-care group. *What could go wrong?*

Well, a lot as it turned out.

One night in late March, just as I was nodding off to sleep in Oakland about 10 PM, a trans woman member felt safe enough to post: *I'm trans. Ask me anything.* What followed was an all-night attack on this poor woman by certain members who were filled with vitriol and out and out hatred. It was basically a war for several hours, as other members rallied to the trans woman's side while she patiently explained who she was and what her life was like.

I woke up to the wreckage the next morning. I had a text from my former publicist. She wrote: *If you haven't looked in on your group, get in there now!* A sick feeling spread through me as I clicked in and found ninety-two member-reported complaints. It was the first time I'd ever gotten any.

So began my trial by fire. It was time to put on my big girl pants and actually lead this thing.

I looked through the trans woman's post as overwhelm flooded my brain. I just wanted to erase the whole thing, as if it had never happened. I really had no idea what else to do. So before I could think it through, I pushed the delete button, effectively removing the post and the several hundred comments that followed.

Immediately I realized my mistake. Now I had no way to track and remove the haters in the group. Nor did I understand how to reverse my action. Nor did I even know the name of the poor trans woman who'd been attacked. Meanwhile, all over the discussion board, angry posts immediately began popping up.

They wanted to know why the thread had been taken down —including all the positive, supportive comments? Did this mean it wasn't safe to be a trans woman here? Did it mean that Suzanne, herself, was a hater?

I knew this group was too good to be true, so I'm outta here, one woman wrote. She got several hundred likes.

Others were demanding I step up and make my policy clear on whether this group admitted people who were trans or non-gender conforming. I began commenting on each post apologetically as fast as I could, trying to keep a lid on the unraveling disaster I had on my hands. *This needs to be made clear to the entire group, Suzanne,* wrote one angry commenter.

So I wrote a post making my policy clear that of course we welcomed trans women and gender non-conforming people in the group, and I pinned it to the top of the feed.

FYI—this is a group about self-love, compassion, kindness, and empathy first for ourselves…then for others. This is not a place for anyone to hate, bully or disrespect, as stated in the rules.

For the record, Trans women are welcome right along with everyone else.

If this is uncomfortable or offensive to you, you have a choice. You can stay, not to bully or offend, but to learn about how a person different from you might think and feel. Or, of course, you can remove yourself from the group, and we thank you for checking the group out and wish you well.

Now I'm going to go meditate!

I attached a picture of Teal with a quote from one of her journals: *Be someone who loves loving yourself.*

Slowly, the ship began to right itself. But then a post appeared from the trans woman herself, complaining that she'd spent the entire night educating people on being trans, only to have her post removed. She was furious. And that's when I snapped.

My self-care group actually wasn't the forum for educating folks on being trans, as important as that point may be to make to society at large. But rather than explain my POV to her, I hit Delete and Block Member, removing her from the group and my world.

It hadn't even occurred to me that we could start a discussion about what had happened, or process this as a group. Or that the trans woman's comment might give me a chance to clarify my position a little more to the members. My German Soldier was now squarely in charge, and she wasn't bothering with feelings like empathy or compassion.

Honestly, I had no idea how else to handle this. Nor did I have any idea what I was doing.

I wondered how long it would take to figure this out.

CHAPTER TWENTY-TWO

I t was the last conscious morning of Teal's life.

She and her housemate Adam occupied the late morning shift in the kitchen in her latest home, this one on Monterey Boulevard in San Francisco. By then, the other techie housemates and their girlfriends were gone to corporate for the day. The kitchen was their common room. A place for coffee and toast, and random, ten-minute conversations about life.

At this hour of the day, both were mostly trying to wake up. Eight hours earlier Adam had returned from his shift as a late-night bartender. And Teal had just woken from the ten-hour sleep her epilepsy demanded every night. A major seizure seemed imminent, but she tried to push that from her mind.

The last thing she wanted to do was to seize in front of her new roommate Adam. Or for him to think she was strange or impaired.

They'd been sharing the apartment for about a month at this point, slowly getting to know each other as housemates do. And they'd been edging toward a shared appreciation for common things, including buttered cinnamon raisin toast and Bob Dylan's iconic blues tune, "Meet Me in the Morning." She liked him.

To Adam, there was something remarkably reassuring about Teal. She drifted in with her guitar and her nose hoop one day, the sort of free spirit San Francisco was once famous for. In this rapidly changing city, she was a type that had all but disappeared.

"What are you doing today?" he asked her as he poured his first cup of coffee.

"Raising money on the street for Planned Parenthood," she replied. But then, that was perfect, he thought. Of course she was raising money with Planned Parenthood. What else would she be doing? Adam took another sip of coffee.

With a light touch, Teal kept inserting ideas into their morning chats. They were unusual ideas, like trusting in the Universe—not the easy, Hallmark cards version but for real. Then there were Teal's thoughts about the afterlife. Clearly, she'd read about it extensively, considered it carefully and believed in it fully. Today she floated the idea that the afterlife was so amazing…well, she, personally, wasn't afraid to die when the time came.

"I think it's probably pretty great up there," Teal asserted.

Adam sipped his coffee thoughtfully. Having been raised by hippie parents with no religious affiliation, Adam had no point of view about the afterlife. All he knew was that eventually everyone was going to die. As far as what happened next, well, that was a crapshoot.

"How do you know?" he asked.

"I just know," Teal said nonchalantly.

Pouring herself a little more coffee, she sat down across from him. "Bottom line is we don't have to be afraid," she said. "At least, that's what I think."

"Yeah, it all sounds good, but…" He smiled, not wanting to throw cold water on her ideas.

She gave him a wry look. "You never know, Adam. You might actually like it."

He chuckled. "I'll keep it in mind, Teal."

A little while later when he left the apartment, Adam felt remarkably lighter. It was how it always was when he hung out with Teal. There was that particular feeling, a comforting positivity.

Like a little bit of her light had somehow rubbed off on him.

Three days after the debacle in my Facebook group, I sat in a Zoom room waiting for my next potential moderator to show.

Soon after the troubles began, I put up a request for volunteer moderators. Finally, I'd gotten around to reading Facebook's group moderation guidelines, and this suggestion was at the top of the list.

Surely there had to be women in this group who would help me scan the posts and comments, weeding those that broke the rules about no self-promotion, politics or bullying. Ideally, they'd also know a lot more than me about how this group admin thing was actually done. Immediately, my request for help was met with a dozen or so interested parties. I requested Zoom chats with each of them, just to make sure we jived.

By now it was late in the afternoon. Mercifully, the first four women I'd talked with were an excellent fit, most of whom had already done this work in other groups. Every one of them exuded competence, and all of them were game to begin moderating immediately. I began to feel some relief for the first time all week.

Now my next prospect, a woman named Tamela Gordon, entered the room. I'd been wanting to meet Tamela, whose email address began with the phrase 'shewritestolive.' *A woman after my heart,* I thought. She ran a successful book group on Facebook for Black women and knew far more than I did about this entire admin thing.

Can't wait to meet you, I wrote to her, when I sent the link for our meeting.

Looking forward to it! she responded.

A large Black woman dressed in a bright yellow camisole appeared and her beaming smile lit up the entire screen. Immediately I could tell she had a fun, joyful vibration, and I smiled back at her. "You look like you're in a warm place," I began.

"Miami," she said. We made some small talk, getting to

know each other. But then after a bit, Tamela grew serious. She gave me a pointed look.

"You know, Suzanne, that trans woman you removed? She went and joined another group," she said. "You know what it's called?"

My stomach tightened. I was so hoping I wasn't going to have to relive all the hell of the past several days. And yet, that was why we were here. She wasn't wrong to bring it up.

"No."

"Inclusive Self-Care," she said. "I joined it, too."

"Ah," I said, my stomach knotting just a little more. *God, please help me*, I prayed.

"I also write about self-care," she continued, "but I'm all about intersectionality. My work is for Black and Brown women, queers, plus-size people—all those folks who get left behind. Because self-care for Black women? It's entirely different from self-care for white women. And fat women can't even fit in conventional bathtubs, you know. So forget the long, hot bath, right?"

She paused, to see if I was taking in what she was saying.

"Okay," I said, nodding for her to continue. My heart and soul were now telling me to shut up and listen. I knew I needed to hear every word she was saying.

"Removing the trans woman was a mistake, Suzanne," she continued.

"I know, I know," I admitted, and I told her I was sorry to have offended people. "Listen, Tamela—seriously, I have no idea what I'm doing."

She nodded wearily in agreement. That much was clear.

Now a wave of emotion swept through me, and I found myself dangerously close to tears. "See here's the thing," I continued, "I've got to get this group right. It's my daughter's legacy," I said. I found myself crying as I explained who Teal was.

"Six months before she died, she wrote me this letter telling me we were supposed to be leaders in light…and…and…this is it, Tamela," I said, my voice breaking. "This group *is* the light leadership. I know it is. But I need help. I can't do it alone. I don't want to screw this up," I emphasized.

Tamela softened visibly. "Ah, okay," she said gently.

"Here's the thing," she continued. "You can't just take down posts and kick people out like that unless you explain to the group what you're doing. There has to be some transparency. Even when you're justified."

Transparency? The thought hadn't even occurred to me.

"You see what happens in situations like this," she pointed out. "People go crazy, and that is anything but self-care, Suzanne." She was right, of course.

Tamela carried on. "Inclusivity means, yeah, we get rid of the haters, but we also talk about things as a group. We have differing points of view. We *learn* from each other." She emphasized the word 'learn.'

My mind was now being blown away. Thousands of women of all different races, ethnicities, sexual identities *learning from each other.* The idea was stunning.

This was, of course, just the type of healing that Teal had intended.

"When there's no accountability, no explanation for what's going on, the marginalized women don't feel safe. Hell, no one feels safe," she said. "People become afraid to even post." Tamela continued. "And you don't want that."

Now she paused. "You may notice the Black women in this group don't post that much." It was true. Even though I was admitting plenty of Black and Brown women every day we seldom heard from them. "They're waiting to see if it's safe," she explained.

We ended up talking for more than an hour that day, and by the end of the call, it was clear to me. Tamela knew things I was never going to know about how the rest of the world—the world that didn't look like me or live like me—thought and felt. And she knew how to manage this group so that *all* the women in it would be treated fairly, equally, and with respect.

My job now was to take a back seat and become a very good student. As it turned out, Tamela has done inclusivity training for other Facebook groups, so I hired her on the spot to train our new crew of moderators. That way we could all get on the same page together from the beginning.

Before the call ended, I made her an offer. "Admin this group with me. Share the whole damn thing with me," I said. Then I added, "If you want to." As it turned out, she did.

Immediately, I thought of videos. I'd set up the group with a no video rule, to prevent people from posting self-promotion videos, live feeds of church services and such. Yet, I'd reserved the right for myself to post videos and Facebook Live feeds about self-care, few of which I'd actually done. Now I invited Tamela to join me in that effort.

Quickly, we began to click along in perfect sync, brainstorming different topics for live streams and ways we could really serve the group best separately and together. In the coming weeks, Tamela and I talked a lot on Zoom. A redo on the rules was mapped out, which took care of a new problem. More and more women were posting about things like child custody, upcoming surgeries, or self-harm. These were topics best left to the professionals, we agreed, no matter how great their need was to discuss them.

So we created a rule that posts needed to be about self-care. That we were unable to facilitate legal, financial, and mental health issues. And we set out to iron out the wrinkles in the way I'd originally set up the group.

Wearing a chakra crown of rainbow crystals on her head, Tamela led our team of ten moderators in two inclusive moderation trainings. She talked about how to gracefully turn off commenting on a controversial post after putting up a comment explaining why. And how to manage those whose comments might be misunderstood. There were neuro-divergent members among us, she pointed out, who might express things differently.

"There has to be engagement, conversation," she insisted. It wasn't fair, she noted, when people were having a conflict and we just took down the whole thing. "It looks like we're picking sides," she said. "Give them space to talk it out. Remind them to be kind. And if they can't, then we step in, explain we're turning off commenting because of too much conflict. If we can leave up examples of people working things out together, they'll get it eventually."

This was a new way of thinking for me. Mainly because I'd assiduously avoided conflict my entire life. Now Tamela was asking me to monitor it, and even embrace it. And I could actually see the logic of this.

Another thing about Tamela was that she kept promoting my self-care book in her own videos. I was grateful, and even struck by this. But she kept telling me I was being too modest about my work. That I needed to post a lot more videos myself and really be all over this group with my presence.

I thanked her for the encouragement I knew I needed, and she laughed. "Think of it this way," she said. "I'm like Don Lemon to your Mike Tyson."

I knew she was right. I *was* still being too damn shy to really be this leader of light I so wanted to be. My own guidance was not to wave my flag too wildly, but to be fairly quiet and let Spirit guide me just where I was meant to go.

Or at least that's what I told myself. For in truth, I hadn't yet fully crawled out from behind the protective rock I'd lived behind since Teal's death. I was almost out as a leader of light, but not completely.

I could still feel myself hanging back a little, though I had no idea why. As if in answer to this, Tamela posted a meme she created a little while later.

The strong survive and the vulnerable fucking thrive.

As usual, she was telling me just what I needed to hear.

Months later when I looked back at the training videos we'd done with Tamela, I could see the anxiety on my face. I had the earnest demeanor of a person terrified of making a mistake. I could remember how incredibly scared I was about the group at the time. *I had to get this right.*

Since then, something new had happened. I'd relaxed and opened up. And I'd gotten perspective.

Now I could see how pointless all my worrying had been. And how the world didn't end even when I did make a mistake. Feelings had been hurt and members removed, while several hundred left of their own accord after the debacle with the trans woman. Yet, life went on. Beautifully, in fact.

The group climbed to 55,000, where it stayed after it stopped being recommended by Facebook. It was unclear why that particular engine had stopped, but it made no difference. Now members referred their friends and others found us simply be searching for 'self-care' in groups.

Six months after the group's massive surge, we'd settled into a quiet, loving place of give and take. Engagement remained high. More than 20,000 members were still checking in every day, reading and posting. Member-reported complaints no longer happened and the spats women got into had largely disappeared. The vibe remained loving and kind. These women genuinely cared about each other.

My so called 'mistake' had led to overall improvement. So what had I been so worried about? My lifelong habit of hiding from life was rapidly disappearing.

I thought of some words from Teal that I'd channeled in the months immediately following her death. At the time, they seemed slightly incomprehensible, as if my brain was just too clouded by grief to understand fully.

Do not judge death with the same limited mind that can barely comprehend the potential in life. You feel that potential sometimes in life's magic—the touch of a lover's hand. The triumph of a long-held dream. The laughter of your child.

But you are afraid of that power, and so you hang back.

Do not hang back. Instead, become quieter and quieter until you are fully suffused with the power and majesty of the God who lives inside of you. Then let go. Do what you want. Allow yourself to truly feel your own deep, soaring magnificence.

The God-given gift of life is available to all who do not fear death.

A loss is only temporary, a fleeting stab of pain. But life is yours to celebrate in each minute of every day.

I realized I knew exactly what she was talking about now.
My life *was* mine to celebrate.
Every minute and every day.

CHAPTER TWENTY-THREE

On the ninth anniversary of Teal's death, I did what I always did. My wife had taught me about the Jewish tradition of lighting Yahrzeit candles on the day a loved one died. So that morning, I lit a candle and placed it on our mantle beside one of my favorite pictures of Teal.

It was a close up, and she was looking out at the camera, her expression knowing. She was smiling slightly and her teal-blue eye gazed out beneath the brush of her bangs appraisingly. As if to say, *Don't you realize you can't hide from me?*

Deborah and I stood there together in our living room, holding hands, saying a small prayer for the love that still flowed from that faraway place where Teal now resided. As usual, I felt her presence around me. Her essence was far less dramatic and far more grounded now. The wild, laughing whoosh of sparkling energy had become a quiet sense of reassurance, an easy comfort.

Yet it was still every bit as real.

"Thank you," I prayed. "Thank you for being here with me, honey."

The energy within me intensified just a bit. A flame glowing just a bit more brightly.

A little while later I sat down to my emails. That morning

my ezine had gone out with the subject line: *Are Angels Really Around Us?* In it, I featured a blog post I'd written about all the different ways I'd experienced Teal around me over the years since her death. And the mental space I had to be in to make that happen.

It wasn't a mindset of fear, anxiety, or sobbing grief. Instead, it was a slightly distracted theta state of calm. Of nothingness. I seemed to achieve it while I was driving, sitting in a bathtub relaxing, or meditating. Or in the still first moments of the day when I lingered in that gorgeous space between sleep and wakefulness. Often it happened in my last dreams of the early morning, just before I awoke.

This was the bridge I traveled to find my way back to my beloved daughter, and I thought about it now as I opened my first email. It was a response to my ezine from one of my readers, a woman who was freshly grieving. Her nineteen-year-old son had been murdered only a few weeks earlier. *Can you help me please?* she wrote, and she included her phone number.

The words of her email were muddled. The sentences ran together in the recognizable tangle of fresh grief. I could feel her excruciating pain. I paused.

Was I actually going to call her?

Was I going to break down the last remains of my wall of self-protection? Was I going to actually reach out share the healing gift I had been given in the most intimate way?

Sure, it was fine to post all sorts of blogs, videos, and podcasts about love and healing, and make speeches and videos about being compassionate. But was I really going to walk the talk where it was needed most? For this was it, here and now. My chance to be an honest-to-God leader in light.

Wasn't *this* the truest expression of everything Teal had been sent to teach me?

It was obvious what I needed to do. I took a breath and dialed her number. The woman picked up after two rings. "Hi," she said, as if she'd been expecting me. Her voice was broken and raw.

"It's Suzanne," I said. And, so, the truest healing began. For her, perhaps.

But most definitely for me.

If this book has touched or healed you, please share it with your hairdresser, your massage therapist, your best friend, your sister, your daughter, your neighbor, your co-workers, and anyone else you know. Let's keep Teal's Unified Field of Love growing.

Thank you.

AFTERWORD

If you are suffering, confused, missing a loved one or longing for connection, Suzanne offers Healing Readings.

Details are at suzannefalter.com/readings, or if you have questions, email Suzanne at suzanne@suzannefalter.com. Offered with love.

Watch Teal sing ... and hear Suzanne and Debi talk about their organ donation experience. suzannefalter.com/free-spirited-extras

RESOURCES

If you feel your finances and your debt are out of control, or you struggle with compulsive spending, financial anorexia, time debting and/or underearning, check out these 12 Step programs for financial well-being:

Debtor's Anonymous (DA): https://debtorsanonymous.org/

Business Debtor's Anonymous (BDA, for business owners) : https://debtorsanonymous.org/getting-started/business-debtors-anonymous/

Underearner's Anonymous (UA): https://www.underearnersanonymous.org/

If you'd like to heal compulsive behavior in love, sex and relationships, visit Sex & Love Addicts Anonymous (SLAA): https://slaafws.org/

ACKNOWLEDGMENTS

Writing this book took more than seven years and at least eight drafts (I lost count, really.) This was mainly due to the fact that I thought the story ended a lot sooner than it did.

Most of the way, I was extensively cheered on and counseled by my literary agent, Annelise Robey, who is godmother to this book. Jane Rotrosen added her expert eye as well. And their loving attention has been a big part of this book's completion.

Because life is life, there were many things that happened along the way that were ultimately not included here due to space and storyline restrictions. So I thank all who read drafts, reminded me of things, told me stories I didn't know, provided feedback, and checked for accuracy along the way. Then there were those who simply offered me support and so became part of the story.

Your loving support and willingness has been a big piece of this book, and I am deeply grateful.

Free Spirited's Earthly helping team includes Micheala McGivern, Alex Forbes, Amera, Gwenn Silva, Rebecca Hurst, Kat Carmichael, Kashi Ananda Devi, Sarah J., Debi Granger, Darla, Didi Stewart, Luke Barns, Sean Davis, Larry Barns, Carmen and Alirio, Dr. Veneeta Singh, Joanne Gregory, Linda Claire Puig, Jon Leland, Robert Weinberg, Kim Osmer, Camille Mumbach, Nacho Valls, Lauren McRay, Bruce and Joan

Stephan, Tamela J. Gordon, Adam Rannels, Nicky Pattinson, Andrea J Lee, Connie, Rose, Kathleen Russell, Rick Morano, Brian Lyttle, Sage Lavine, the ace moderation team of the Self-Care Group for Extremely Busy Women, the late Kristine Louise Phillips, Conscious Girlfriend, the Petaluma Hospice Support Group for Grieving Parents. And, as ever, my fellows in recovery.

My amazing assistant, Danielle Hartman Acee (authorsassistant.com), has shepherded me through this project with great support and patience, and provided design, proofreading and formatting, and excellent feedback. Vanessa Mendozzi provided our beautiful cover. Cover photography is by In Her Image Photography of Petaluma, CA. ww.inherimagephoto.com.

And finally, thank you to my dear wife 'Deborah' with whom life is simply great.

ABOUT THE AUTHOR

Suzanne Falter is a writer, podcaster and speaker whose work has appeared in SELF, O, More, Fitness, New Woman and The New York Times. She is the author of multiple self-help titles including *The Extremely Busy Woman's Guide to Self-Care* (Sourcebooks) and numerous novels. Suzanne also hosts the popular Self-Care for Extremely Busy Women podcast and Facebook group. You can learn more about her work at www.suzannefalter.com.

ALSO BY SUZANNE FALTER

Non-Fiction

The Extremely Busy Women's Guide to Self-Care

The Joy of Letting Go

Surrendering to Joy

How Much Joy Can You Stand?

Living Your Joy

Box of Joy: Three Books About Happiness

Fiction

Drive: An Oaktown Girls Novel

Committed: An Oaktown Girls Novel

Destined: An Oaktown Girls Novel

Revealed: An Oaktown Girls Novel

Undivided: An Oaktown Girls Novel

By Suzanne Falter & Jack Harvey

Transformed; San Francisco

Transformed: Paris

Transformed: POTUS

Printed in Great Britain
by Amazon

19289854R00113